Campbell's

ANNIVERSARY 75th COOKBOOK

Cooking in Minutes

Whether you're busy at home, busy with a career or juggling both, your time for grocery shopping, cooking and cleanup is short. To help you, Campbell's team of experienced home economists has been busy testing and tasting more than 115 timesaving recipes just for you. The result: Campbell's *Cooking in Minutes* cookbook presenting recipes guaranteed to be M'm! M'm! Good!

Campbell Soup Company has been giving cooks the kind of recipe ideas and information they've requested for years. Back in 1916, we published one of our first cookbooks, *Helps for the Hostess*, featuring soup as an ingredient in many of the recipes. The cookbook also shared tips on proper table etiquette, napkin folding and menu ideas. But lifestyles have changed. Convenience, taste and value are more important than ever to today's cooks. Campbell's welcomes you to the 1990s with this 75th anniversary soup cookbook full of beat-the-clock recipes, timesaving tips and easy menu ideas geared to get you in and out of the kitchen—FAST.

The Ultimate Recipe Ingredient
Get a head start in the kitchen and begin with Campbell's condensed soup . . . that's the real secret to making delicious dishes in minutes. Campbell's condensed soups make cooking easy and versatile for new and experienced cooks alike because the rich, delicious flavor eliminates the need for a lot of extra ingredients.

Many of these recipes use budget-easing ingredients for everyday tasty and nourishing meals. Every recipe has been carefully developed and tested by home economists in the Campbell's Creative Food Center ensuring perfect results every time you cook.

Campbell Soup's top-quality standards are reflected in every soup variety and are the beginnings of fabulous meals. There's a wide variety of convenient-to-use cooking soups, from the traditional favorites—cream of mushroom, cream of celery and cream of chicken—to the newer ones—cream of broccoli, nacho cheese and zesty tomato. For a complete line-up, look at the photo of Campbell's Family of Cooking Soups on page 5.

In this fabulous new cookbook, you'll find regional recipe favorites such as spicy Southwestern-style Nacho Chicken Tostadas, Shortcut Brunswick Stew from the South and even a cheesesteak-flavored soup from Philadelphia. For the more adventuresome cook, there's Salsa Swordfish, herbed Vegetable Pilaf and nutty Middle Eastern-Style Dip. Look for the classics, such as Campbell's Classic Glorified Chicken, more popular than ever, which can be made with as many as five different soups, depending on your taste or what's on hand in your cupboard. New Broccoli Bake is similar to classic Green Bean Bake made with cream of mushroom soup but with our newest soup . . . cream of broccoli.

As you turn these pages, look for the step-saving tips designed to speed up meal preparation. Check under the recipe titles for serving ideas geared to make meal planning easy. You'll also find handy ingredient substitutes when you want to change a seasoning or make use of in-season vegetables and herbs. For additional information on ingredient substitutes, refer to the Emergency Substitutions chart on page 5.

Timesaving Symbols

To help you choose the recipe designed for the cooking time you have available, we've divided the main-dish recipes according to the time you need to prepare and cook them. For super-fast recipes, go to the chapter titled 20-Minute Express—each recipe can be prepared and cooked in just 20 minutes. And on days when you have a little more time, try the recipes in the 30-Minute Countdown section. If you choose a main dish from Easy-Going Entrées, give yourself about an hour for assembly and cooking . . . set the table, toss a salad or even kick up your feet and relax while your dinner cooks to perfection. The last two chapters feature fast-cooking side dishes and snacks. Throughout the book, look for these timesaving symbols appearing with many of the recipes.

Microwave: An alternative to conventional cooking when time is of the essence. It's a great way to keep you—and the kitchen—cool during hot weather.

6 Ingredients: Recipes featuring 6 ingredients or less.

Extra-Easy: Fifteen minutes or less to get the ingredients ready to microwave, simmer on the range top or pop in the oven.

Step-saving Tips

Here are nine ways to save time both in the kitchen and at the grocery store. Everyday cooking can be hassle-free when you:

- *Organize your kitchen*
  Store utensils where you use them to save time and steps. Don't clutter up the counter with equipment you rarely use.

  Do keep step-saving appliances handy. Your food processor and blender will help save time if you don't have to pull them from storage to use. Don't let dishes pile up. Clean up after each meal to make your kitchen ideal for timesaving cooking.

- **Keep it easy**
  A quick meal is an easy meal. Depending on how much time you have, choose a main dish from one of the first three chapters. Then add a steamed vegetable, a bowl of soup or toss a green salad with a bottled dressing. If you prefer, start with one of our fast side dishes and broil your favorite fish or meat to go with it. End the meal with some fresh fruit or a refreshing sorbet.

- **Make a grocery list**
  Attach a list of basic ingredients to your refrigerator and note when you're running low. Arrange the items on the list in the order you find them in the supermarket. Check the Food Equivalents Chart on the inside back cover when you're not sure how many lemons you'll need for a cup of juice or how many potatoes are in a pound.

- **Plan by the week**
  Save time by grocery shopping once a week—no extra time lost in lines and unpacking groceries. Stop for perishables only when you need them—you'll be surprised how much time you save.

- **Keep the basics on hand**
  Store the makings of several meals on your shelf and in your refrigerator-freezer: Campbell's soups, packaged rice mixes, bottled salad dressings, frozen vegetables, canned tuna, cheese and assorted condiments to name a few.

- **Buy ingredients conveniently prepared**
  Although it may cost a little more, you can save preparation time if you buy foods the way they'll be used in a recipe. For example, look for shredded cheese, boneless chicken breasts, bread crumbs, chopped nuts and cut-up salad ingredients. When unpacking groceries, store similar items together. Keep special areas on your shelves for Campbell's soups, pasta, canned vegetables, dried legumes, sauce mixes, rice mixes and other favorite staples.

- **Assemble all ingredients**
  Get all the ingredients together before starting to cook. You'll speed up preparation and avoid confusion if you're interrupted.

- **Use spare moments**
  If you're between steps in a recipe, go on to the next step and prepare the ingredients. Or, use the time to steam vegetables or cut up fruit for dessert, for example. Keep up with kitchen cleanup and you won't be left with a mess when dinner is ready.

- **Make extra for later**
  Whenever you cook pasta or rice, cook extra to serve later in a salad or as part of another recipe. Leftover meat is easily turned into another meal—look for the many delicious recipes in this book using cooked chicken, for example.

Campbell's *Cooking in Minutes* cookbook is brimming with recipes and ideas guaranteed to streamline your cooking every day of the week. Enjoy!

EMERGENCY SUBSTITUTIONS

When a recipe calls for:	You may substitute:
1 cup fresh whole milk	1 cup 2%, 1% or skim milk, or ½ cup evaporated milk plus ½ cup water
1 cup half-and-half	1 cup less 2 tablespoons whole milk plus 2 tablespoons melted margarine or butter
1 clove garlic	⅛ teaspoon garlic powder or minced dried garlic
1 small onion	1 teaspoon onion powder or 1 tablespoon minced dried onion, rehydrated
1 teaspoon dry mustard	1 tablespoon prepared mustard
1 tablespoon cornstarch (for thickening)	2 tablespoons all-purpose flour or 2 teaspoons quick-cooking tapioca
1 cup sour cream	1 cup plain yogurt
1 cup sliced zucchini	1 cup sliced summer squash
1 tablespoon chopped fresh herbs	1 teaspoon dried herbs, crushed
½ cup granulated sugar	½ cup packed brown sugar
¼ cup honey	¼ cup light corn syrup

Campbell's Family of Cooking Soups

Chicken-Broccoli Divan

*One of Campbell's most requested recipes! To serve eight,
the recipe can be doubled as in the photo. Pictured
opposite and on front cover.*

1 pound fresh broccoli, cut into
    spears, or 1 package
    (10 ounces) frozen broccoli
    spears, cooked and drained
1½ cups cubed cooked chicken
    or turkey
1 can (10¾ ounces) Campbell's
    condensed cream of broccoli
    or cream of chicken soup

⅓ cup milk
½ cup shredded Cheddar cheese
    (2 ounces)
2 tablespoons fine dry bread
    crumbs
1 tablespoon margarine or
    butter, melted

1. Preheat oven to 450°F.

2. In 10- by 6-inch baking dish, arrange broccoli; top with chicken.
   In small bowl, combine soup and milk; pour over chicken. Sprinkle
   with cheese. In cup, combine bread crumbs and margarine; sprinkle
   over cheese.

3. Bake 15 minutes or until hot and bubbling. Makes 4 servings.

To microwave: Do not cook broccoli. In 10- by 6-inch microwave-safe
baking dish, arrange broccoli. Cover with vented plastic wrap;
microwave on HIGH 6 minutes, rearranging broccoli halfway through
cooking. Drain. Top with chicken. In small bowl, combine soup and
milk; pour over chicken. Sprinkle with cheese. In cup, combine bread
crumbs and margarine; sprinkle over cheese. Cover with waxed paper;
microwave on HIGH 6 minutes or until heated through, rotating dish
halfway through heating.

Chicken-Broccoli Divan

Nacho Chicken Tostadas EXTRA EASY

To serve as shown in the photo, follow directions below for making Tortilla Cups. Pictured opposite.

1 can (11 ounces) Campbell's condensed nacho cheese soup/dip
2½ cups cubed cooked chicken
1 can (8 ounces) stewed tomatoes
1 can (4 ounces) chopped green chilies, drained

10 purchased tostada shells
5 cups shredded lettuce
Chopped sweet red and yellow peppers for garnish
Fresh cilantro or parsley for garnish

1. In 2-quart saucepan over medium heat, combine soup, chicken, tomatoes and chilies; heat through.

2. On each tostada shell, arrange ½ *cup* of the lettuce. Top with ¼ *cup* of the soup mixture. Garnish with red peppers and cilantro. Makes 10 tostadas or 5 servings.

Tortilla Cups: Preheat oven to 400°F. Use 10 (8-inch) corn tortillas instead of tostada shells. On baking sheet, place 5 balls of aluminum foil (about 4-inch diameter). Spray 10-inch nonstick skillet with vegetable cooking spray. Over high heat, heat *one* corn tortilla 5 seconds on each side until tortilla is softened. Drain on paper towels. Immediately drape tortilla over foil ball on baking sheet. Repeat with 4 additional tortillas. Bake 5 minutes or until golden. Remove from oven and cool on foil balls. Turn tortilla cups over; remove foil balls. Repeat with remaining tortillas. Proceed as directed in step 2.
Makes 10 Tortilla Cups.

Easy Basil Chicken with Rice EXTRA EASY

1 can (10½ ounces) Campbell's condensed chicken broth
1 can (16 ounces) stewed tomatoes
2 cloves garlic, minced
1 teaspoon dried basil leaves, crushed

2 cups cubed cooked chicken
1½ cups quick-cooking rice, uncooked
1 cup frozen peas
¼ teaspoon hot pepper sauce

In 3-quart saucepan over high heat, heat broth, tomatoes, garlic and basil to boiling. Add chicken, rice, peas and hot pepper sauce. Return to boiling. Remove from heat. Cover; let stand 5 minutes or until most of the liquid is absorbed. Fluff rice with fork before serving. Makes 5 cups or 4 servings.

Nacho Chicken Tostadas

Spicy Broccoli Beef

If you use fine egg noodles, they'll cook in less time.

1 can (10½ ounces) Campbell's
 condensed beef broth
½ cup water
2 tablespoons cornstarch
1 tablespoon soy sauce
½ teaspoon crushed red pepper
2 tablespoons peanut oil,
 divided

4 cups broccoli flowerets
2 green onions, diagonally
 sliced
1 pound boneless beef sirloin
 steak, thinly sliced
Hot cooked noodles

1. In bowl, combine broth, water, cornstarch, soy sauce and red pepper; set aside.

2. In 10-inch skillet over high heat, in *1 tablespoon* hot oil, stir-fry broccoli and green onions 2 minutes or until tender-crisp. Transfer to bowl.

3. In same skillet over high heat, in remaining hot oil, stir-fry beef *half* at a time, until color just changes. Transfer to bowl with broccoli.

4. Stir broth mixture into skillet. Cook over high heat until mixture boils and thickens, stirring often. Add broccoli-beef mixture; heat through. Serve over noodles. Serve with additional *soy sauce*, if desired. Makes 4 cups or 4 servings.

Skillet Black-Eyed Peas 'n' Rice

For more zip, increase the amount of hot pepper sauce.

1 package (10 ounces) frozen
 chopped spinach
¾ pound bulk pork sausage
1 medium onion, sliced
2 cloves garlic, minced
1 can (10½ ounces) Campbell's
 condensed beef broth

½ cup water
1 can (16 ounces) black-eyed
 peas, drained
1½ cups quick-cooking rice,
 uncooked
¼ teaspoon hot pepper sauce

1. Cook spinach according to package directions; drain well.

2. Meanwhile, in 10-inch skillet over medium heat, cook sausage, onion and garlic until browned, stirring to separate meat. Spoon off fat. Stir in broth, water and peas. Heat to boiling.

3. Stir in rice, cooked spinach and hot pepper sauce. Heat to boiling. Remove from heat. Cover; let stand 5 minutes or until most of the liquid is absorbed. Fluff rice with fork before serving. Makes 6½ cups or 4 servings.

Szechuan Shredded Pork

Stir chopped fresh parsley, coriander or chives into the rice for added color and flavor.

1 1/2 pounds pork shoulder
    blade steak
  1 can (10 3/4 ounces) Campbell's
    condensed golden
    mushroom soup
1/2 cup water
1/4 cup dry sherry
  1 tablespoon soy sauce

1/2 teaspoon ground ginger
1/2 teaspoon crushed red pepper
  2 tablespoons vegetable oil,
    divided
1/2 cup diagonally sliced carrot
1/2 medium sweet red or green
    pepper, cut into 2-inch
    julienne strips
Hot cooked rice

1. Remove bone from steak; thinly slice steak, discarding excess fat. Set aside.

2. In small bowl, combine soup, water, sherry, soy sauce, ginger and crushed red pepper.

3. In 10-inch skillet over high heat, in *1 tablespoon* hot oil, stir-fry carrot and red pepper strips until tender-crisp. Transfer to bowl.

4. In same skillet, in remaining oil, stir-fry pork *half* at a time, until pork is no longer pink. Stir in cooked vegetables and soup mixture. Heat to boiling. Serve over rice. Makes 4 servings.

Speedy Spicy Chili ◆EXTRA EASY◆

Pass bowls of chopped tomato, shredded cheese, sliced green onions and sour cream to add pizzazz to this extra-fast chili.

1 pound ground beef
1/2 cup chopped onion
  1 clove garlic, minced
  1 tablespoon chili powder
  1 can (16 ounces) pork and
    beans in tomato sauce

1 can (10 3/4 ounces) Campbell's
    condensed tomato soup
1 can (4 ounces) chopped
    green chilies
1/2 cup water

1. In 10-inch skillet over medium-high heat, cook beef, onion, garlic and chili powder until beef is browned and onion is tender, stirring to separate meat. Spoon off fat.

2. Stir in beans, soup, chilies and water. Heat to boiling. Reduce heat to low. Simmer 10 minutes, stirring occasionally. Makes 4 cups or 4 servings.

Cod Steaks Oriental

Use fresh spinach leaves instead of bok choy if you prefer—just shred coarsely with a sharp knife. Pictured opposite.

$1/2$ pound bok choy
2 tablespoons cornstarch
2 tablespoons teriyaki sauce
2 tablespoons dry sherry
1 can ($10^{1}/2$ ounces) Campbell's condensed chicken broth
4 green onions, cut into 2-inch diagonal pieces
1 cup sweet red pepper cut into 1-inch strips
$1/8$ teaspoon crushed red pepper
4 cod or halibut steaks, cut $3/4$ inch thick (about 2 pounds)

1. Cut bok choy stems into $1/4$-inch slices; coarsely shred leaves. In cup, stir together cornstarch, teriyaki sauce and sherry until well blended. Set aside.

2. In 10-inch skillet over high heat, combine broth, green onions, red pepper strips, crushed red pepper and bok choy stems. Heat to boiling. Arrange fish over vegetable mixture. Reduce heat to low. Cover; cook 8 to 12 minutes or until fish flakes easily when tested.

3. Transfer fish to platter; keep warm. Stir cornstarch mixture and bok choy leaves into skillet. Cook over high heat until mixture boils and thickens, stirring often. Spoon over fish. Makes 4 servings.

Fettuccine with Mushroom-Clam Sauce

Look for fresh or refrigerated pasta at your supermarket—most cook in 5 minutes or less. You'll need about 8 ounces for 4 servings.

2 cans ($6^{1}/2$ ounces *each*) chopped clams
1 tablespoon margarine or butter
2 cloves garlic, minced
$1/4$ cup Chablis or other dry white wine
1 can ($10^{3}/4$ ounces) Campbell's condensed cream of mushroom soup
$1/4$ cup grated Parmesan cheese
Hot cooked fettuccine
Chopped fresh parsley for garnish

1. Drain clams, reserving liquid. In 2-quart saucepan over medium heat, in hot margarine, cook garlic until golden, stirring often.

2. Add clam liquid and wine. Increase heat to high. Boil 6 minutes or until liquid is reduced to $1/2$ cup.

3. Stir in soup, clams and Parmesan. Reduce heat to low. Simmer 3 minutes or until heated through, stirring occasionally. Serve over fettuccine. Garnish with parsley. Makes 4 servings.

Cod Steaks Oriental

Saucy Cheese Tortellini

1 pound fresh or frozen cheese
tortellini
1 can (10¾ ounces) Campbell's
condensed cream of
mushroom soup
1 soup can milk
¾ cup frozen peas
½ cup shredded carrot

⅛ teaspoon freshly ground
pepper
3 tablespoons grated Parmesan
cheese
¼ cup chopped fresh parsley
Chopped toasted walnuts for
garnish

1. Cook tortellini according to package directions; drain.

2. Meanwhile, in 3-quart saucepan, combine soup, milk, peas, carrot and pepper. Over medium heat, heat to boiling. Reduce heat to low. Cover; simmer 4 minutes or until peas are tender, stirring occasionally.

3. Stir in Parmesan and parsley. Heat until cheese melts. Stir in cooked tortellini. Garnish with walnuts. Makes 5 cups or 4 servings.

> **Walnuts are easy to toast** in your microwave oven. Arrange
> on a paper towel; microwave on HIGH 45 seconds or
> until lightly browned.

Classic Campbelled Eggs

Make with cream of celery, Cheddar cheese, cream of mushroom or nacho cheese soup for a change of pace.

1 can (10¾ ounces) Campbell's
condensed cream of
chicken soup
8 eggs, beaten
Dash pepper

2 tablespoons margarine
or butter
Chopped fresh parsley or
chives for garnish

1. In medium bowl, stir soup until smooth. Gradually blend in eggs and pepper.

2. In 10-inch skillet over low heat, melt margarine. Pour in egg mixture. As eggs begin to set, stir lightly so uncooked egg flows to bottom. Cook until set but still very moist. Garnish with parsley. Serve immediately. Makes 4 servings.

To microwave: Omit margarine. In 3-quart microwave-safe casserole, stir soup until smooth. Gradually blend in eggs and pepper. Cover with lid; microwave on HIGH 6½ minutes or until eggs are nearly set, stirring 3 times during cooking. Let stand, covered, 2 minutes. Garnish with parsley.

Hamburger 'n' Fixings Sandwiches 〰

Serve an assortment of toppers with this sandwich: chopped onion, leaf lettuce, pickle relish and sliced tomatoes.

1 pound ground beef
4 hard rolls (*each* 8 inches long), split lengthwise
1 can (10½ ounces) Campbell's condensed French onion soup
¼ cup ketchup
2 tablespoons finely chopped sweet pickle
2 teaspoons spicy brown mustard
⅛ teaspoon pepper

1. In 10-inch skillet over medium heat, cook beef until browned, stirring to separate meat. Spoon off fat. Meanwhile, toast hard rolls.

2. Stir soup, ketchup, pickle, mustard and pepper into skillet. Heat to boiling. Reduce heat to low; heat through. Spoon about ½ cup of the beef mixture onto each roll bottom. Top with desired toppings; adjust roll tops. Makes 4 servings.

To microwave: In 2-quart microwave-safe casserole, crumble beef. Cover with lid; microwave on HIGH 5 minutes or until beef is no longer pink, stirring once during cooking to separate meat. Spoon off fat. Meanwhile, toast rolls. Stir soup, ketchup, pickle, mustard and pepper into casserole. Microwave, uncovered, on HIGH 3 to 4 minutes or until hot and bubbling, stirring 3 times during cooking. Serve as directed in step 2.

Reuben-Style Skillet ◆*EXTRA EASY*◆

This flavorful skillet dish will remind you of a classic Reuben sandwich, minus the sauerkraut. Use coleslaw mix to save valuable chopping time.

1 can (10¾ ounces) Campbell's condensed cream of potato soup
2 tablespoons Thousand Island salad dressing
½ cup water
3 cups purchased fresh coleslaw mix
2 cups cooked corned beef cut into 2-inch julienne strips
2 cups plain croutons
1 cup shredded Swiss cheese (4 ounces)
2 tablespoons chopped fresh parsley

1. In 10-inch skillet, combine soup, dressing and water. Over high heat, heat to boiling. Stir in coleslaw mix. Reduce heat to low. Cover; simmer 5 minutes or until cabbage is tender-crisp, stirring twice.

2. Stir in beef. Cover; cook 2 minutes or until heated, stirring once.

3. Combine croutons, cheese and parsley. Sprinkle over mixture; heat 2 minutes or until cheese melts. Makes 4 servings.

Easy Turkey Salad

For a no-fuss, keep-cool meal, add a cluster of red grapes and sesame crackers. Pictured opposite.

1 can (10¾ ounces) Campbell's
  condensed cream of
  celery soup
½ cup mayonnaise
4 cups chopped cooked turkey
1 cup finely chopped celery

½ cup chopped sweet red pepper
½ cup sliced green onions
2 tablespoons chopped fresh
  parsley
⅛ teaspoon pepper
  Leaf lettuce

In large bowl, stir together soup and mayonnaise until smooth. Fold in turkey, celery, red pepper, onions, parsley and pepper. Serve mixture on leaf lettuce. Cover and refrigerate any remaining salad mixture. Makes about 5 cups or 8 servings.

Pepperoni Pizza Soup

This spicy pizza soup uses the family-sized 26-ounce can of condensed tomato soup. For 2 servings, follow directions below using a 10¾-ounce can of tomato soup.

1 can (26 ounces) Campbell's
  condensed tomato soup
1 soup can water
⅔ cup sliced pepperoni

1 teaspoon dried Italian
  seasoning, crushed
  Shredded mozzarella cheese
  Croutons

In 2-quart saucepan, combine soup, water, pepperoni and Italian seasoning. Over medium heat, heat through. Serve topped with cheese and croutons. Makes 6 cups or 4 servings.

Variation: Substitute ½ pound cooked, drained ground beef for pepperoni.

Pepperoni Pizza Soup for Two: In 1-quart saucepan, combine 1 can (10¾ ounces) Campbell's condensed tomato soup, 1 soup can water, ⅓ cup sliced pepperoni and ½ teaspoon dried Italian seasoning, crushed. Proceed as directed above. Makes 2½ cups or 2 servings.

Easy Turkey Salad

Tuna-Tortellini Soup *EXTRA EASY*

Next time use canned, cooked chunk chicken. Pictured opposite.

1 can (10¾ ounces) Campbell's condensed cream of broccoli soup
1 can (10½ ounces) Campbell's condensed chicken broth
1 cup water
¼ teaspoon dried basil leaves, crushed
⅛ teaspoon garlic powder

2 cups fresh or frozen cheese tortellini
1 cup frozen whole kernel corn
1 cup milk
1 can (6½ ounces) tuna, drained
2 tablespoons diced pimento
Chopped fresh parsley for garnish

1. In 3-quart saucepan, combine soup, broth, water, basil and garlic. Cover; over high heat, heat to boiling.

2. Add tortellini and corn. Reduce heat to low. Cover; simmer 10 minutes or until tortellini is tender.

3. Stir in milk, tuna and pimento; heat through. Garnish with parsley. Makes 6 cups or 4 servings.

Creamy Shrimp Bisque

2 tablespoons margarine or butter
1 cup sliced fresh mushrooms
2 tablespoons sliced green onion
1 clove garlic, minced
1 can (10½ ounces) Campbell's condensed chicken broth

1 pound frozen shelled and deveined medium shrimp
3 tablespoons all-purpose flour
½ cup light cream
⅓ cup Chablis or other dry white wine
1 tablespoon chopped fresh parsley

1. In 10-inch skillet over medium heat, in hot margarine, cook mushrooms, green onion and garlic until tender, stirring occasionally. Add broth and shrimp. Heat to boiling.

2. Meanwhile, in cup, stir together flour and cream until well blended. Stir into broth mixture. Cook until mixture boils and thickens, stirring often.

3. Add wine and parsley; heat through. Makes 4 cups or 4 servings.

Tuna-Tortellini Soup

Spicy Bean Soup

Serve this hearty vegetable soup with tortilla chips,
warm flour tortillas or purchased corn muffins.
Pictured opposite.

1 tablespoon vegetable oil
½ cup chopped green pepper
½ cup chopped onion
1 can (10¾ ounces) Campbell's
   condensed tomato soup
1 can (19 ounces) chick peas
   (garbanzo beans), drained

1 can (16 ounces) black beans,
   drained
1 soup can water
1 teaspoon Worcestershire sauce
⅛ teaspoon hot pepper sauce
1 cup shredded Cheddar or
   Monterey Jack cheese
   (4 ounces)

1. In 3-quart saucepan over medium heat, in hot oil, cook green pepper
   and onion 5 minutes, stirring occasionally.

2. Stir in soup, chick peas, beans, water, Worcestershire and hot
   pepper sauce. Heat to boiling. Reduce heat to low. Cover; simmer
   5 minutes, stirring occasionally. Serve topped with cheese. Makes
   6 cups or 4 servings.

For a warm bread super-fast, wrap flour tortillas in plain white
paper towels. Microwave on HIGH 30 seconds.

Knockwurst Potato Chowder

2 tablespoons margarine
   or butter
3 knockwurst, cut into ¼-inch
   slices (about 9 ounces)
½ cup finely chopped celery
1 medium onion, finely
   chopped

2 cans (10¾ ounces *each*)
   Campbell's condensed
   cream of potato soup
1 soup can milk
1 cup water
½ cup frozen whole kernel corn
2 tablespoons chopped
   fresh parsley

1. In 4-quart saucepan over high heat, in hot margarine, cook
   knockwurst, celery and onion until sausage is browned, stirring
   occasionally. Spoon off fat.

2. Stir in soup, milk, water and corn. Heat to boiling. Reduce heat to
   low. Cover; simmer 4 minutes or until corn is tender. Stir in parsley.
   Makes 6¾ cups or 4 servings.

Spicy Bean Soup

Smoked Turkey Bean Soup

Next time use leftover roast turkey or baked ham instead of the smoked turkey breast.

1 tablespoon vegetable oil
1 medium onion, chopped
2 cloves garlic, minced
1 can (10¾ ounces) Campbell's condensed cream of potato soup
1 can (16 ounces) white cannellini beans, drained

1 soup can water
¼ pound smoked turkey breast, cut into ½-inch pieces (about 1 cup)
1 teaspoon paprika
1 tablespoon chopped fresh parsley

1. In 2-quart saucepan over medium heat, in hot oil, cook onion and garlic until tender, stirring occasionally.

2. Stir in soup, beans, water, turkey and paprika. Heat to boiling. Reduce heat to low. Simmer 5 minutes. Stir in parsley. Makes 4½ cups or 3 servings.

Chicken 'n' Shrimp Gumbo

If you're short on time, use two cans (5 ounces each) cooked chunk chicken.

1 can (8 ounces) tomatoes, undrained, cut up
1 tablespoon margarine or butter
½ cup sliced green onions
2 cloves garlic, minced
2 cans (10¾ ounces *each*) Campbell's condensed chicken gumbo soup

1 can (10¾ ounces) Campbell's condensed cream of chicken soup
1 cup chopped cooked chicken
1 teaspoon hot pepper sauce
1 pound frozen shelled and deveined medium shrimp
3 cups hot cooked rice

1. Drain tomatoes, reserving liquid. Add enough water to make *1 cup*; set aside.

2. Meanwhile, in 4-quart saucepan over medium heat, in hot margarine, cook green onions and garlic until onions are tender, stirring occasionally.

3. Add both soups, stirring until smooth. Gradually add tomatoes, reserved liquid, chicken and hot pepper sauce. Cover; heat to boiling.

4. Add shrimp. Reduce heat to low. Cover; cook 8 minutes or until shrimp are pink and opaque, stirring occasionally. Spoon ½ cup of the rice into each soup bowl; top with about *1½ cups* of the soup. Makes 8 cups or 5 servings.

Country Ham 'n' Potato Soup

For a change of pace, try other vegetables instead of cabbage, such as: chopped bok choy, romaine or spinach.

1 tablespoon margarine
 or butter
1 cup shredded cabbage
1/4 pound fully cooked ham,
 cut into strips
 (1 cup)

1 can (10¾ ounces) Campbell's
 condensed cream of
 potato soup
1 soup can water
1 tablespoon chopped fresh
 parsley

1. In 2-quart saucepan over medium-high heat, in hot margarine, cook cabbage and ham 5 minutes or until cabbage is tender, stirring occasionally.

2. Stir in remaining ingredients. Heat to boiling. Reduce heat to low; heat through. Makes 3½ cups or 2 servings.

Philadelphia Cheesesteak Soup

Here's a spin-off of the popular Philadelphia cheesesteak sandwich. If you like, stir in some sliced hot Italian peppers—that's how many Philadelphians enjoy their cheesesteaks.

2 frozen chipped beef sandwich
 steaks (2 ounces *each*)
2 tablespoons margarine
 or butter
1 medium onion, cut into
 thin wedges
1/2 small green pepper,
 cut into strips

1 can (11 ounces) Campbell's
 condensed Cheddar cheese
 soup/sauce
1 cup water
1 teaspoon Worcestershire
 sauce
1½ cups toasted bread cubes
 (about 1 inch)

1. Cut each steak into 2- by ½-inch strips.

2. In 3-quart saucepan over medium heat, in hot margarine, cook onion and green pepper until tender, stirring occasionally. Add steak strips; cook meat until color just changes, stirring often.

3. Stir in soup until smooth. Gradually stir in water and Worcestershire; heat through. Serve topped with toasted bread cubes. Makes 3 cups or 2 servings.

> ***Toast bread cubes** under the broiler. Or use purchased seasoned croutons.*

Flash-in-the-pan skillet meals, fast-fixin' main dishes and snappy stir-fries ready to eat in 30 minutes or less—

Salsa Swordfish

Serve steamed fresh asparagus spears for a quick and colorful accompaniment. Pictured opposite.

1 can (10¾ ounces) Campbell's
    condensed tomato soup
½ cup salsa
2 teaspoons chopped fresh
    cilantro or 1 tablespoon
    chopped fresh parsley

2 teaspoons lemon juice
4 swordfish steaks,
    cut ¾ to 1 inch thick
    (about 2 pounds)
Fresh cilantro or parsley
    for garnish

1. In 10-inch skillet, combine soup, salsa, cilantro and lemon juice. Over high heat, heat to boiling. Arrange steaks in soup mixture. Return to boiling. Reduce heat to low. Cover; simmer 15 minutes or until fish flakes easily when tested with fork.

2. Transfer fish to platter; keep warm. Over medium heat, cook sauce until slightly thickened, stirring occasionally. Serve sauce over fish. Garnish with cilantro. Makes 4 servings.

Dijon Cod Fillets

For a quick-fix vegetable, stir-fry sliced broccoli stems and drizzle with a squeeze of fresh lemon.

1 pound cod fillets, cut ½ to
    ¾ inch thick
2 tablespoons margarine
    or butter
1 cup diagonally sliced carrot
1 small onion, finely chopped

¼ cup water
1 can (10¾ ounces) Campbell's
    condensed cream of celery
    soup
2 teaspoons Dijon-style mustard
⅛ teaspoon pepper

1. Preheat oven to 400°F. Arrange fish in 12- by 8-inch baking dish. Bake 10 minutes.

2. Meanwhile, in 2-quart saucepan over medium heat, in hot margarine, cook carrot and onion 3 minutes, stirring occasionally. Add water. Cover; cook 5 minutes or until carrot is tender.

3. In bowl, combine soup, mustard and pepper. Spoon over fish. Bake 10 minutes more or until fish flakes easily when tested with fork. Transfer fish to platter. Stir sauce; spoon over fish. Makes 4 servings.

Salsa Swordfish

ny Dill Salmon Steaks

*Purchase a seasoned wild rice combo to serve with this fish—
many cook in just 10 minutes.*

1 tablespoon margarine
   or butter
½ cup chopped green onions
1 can (10¾ ounces) Campbell's
   condensed cream of
   celery soup
½ cup half-and-half

2 tablespoons Chablis or other
   dry white wine
2 tablespoons chopped fresh
   dill or 1 teaspoon dried dill
   weed, crushed
4 salmon steaks, cut 1 inch
   thick (about 2 pounds)

1. In 10-inch skillet over medium heat, in hot margarine, cook green onions until tender, stirring often. Add soup, half-and-half, wine and dill; stir until smooth.

2. Arrange fish steaks in soup mixture. Heat to boiling. Reduce heat to low. Cover; simmer 15 minutes or until fish flakes easily when tested with fork. Makes 4 servings.

To microwave: In 12- by 8-inch microwave-safe baking dish, combine margarine and green onions. Cover with vented plastic wrap; microwave on HIGH 2 minutes or until onions are tender, stirring once during cooking. Add soup, half-and-half, wine and dill; stir until smooth. Arrange fish steaks in dish with thicker portions of fish toward outside of dish. Cover; microwave on HIGH 10 to 11 minutes or until fish flakes easily when tested with fork, rotating dish twice during cooking. Let stand, covered, 5 minutes before serving.

Fish with Swiss Cheese Sauce

Drizzle sliced cucumbers and onions with a tangy vinaigrette for an easy, great-tasting salad that complements this fish dish.

6 flounder fillets, cut about
   ¼ inch thick (about
   1½ pounds)
1 can (10¾ ounces) Campbell's
   condensed cream of
   mushroom soup

2 tablespoons Chablis or other
   dry white wine
½ cup shredded Swiss cheese
   (2 ounces)
1 tablespoon chopped fresh
   parsley

1. Preheat oven to 400°F. In 13- by 9-inch baking dish, arrange fish fillets in a single layer. Bake 10 minutes.

2. Meanwhile, in small bowl, combine soup and wine. Pour soup mixture over fillets, stirring into cooking liquid. Sprinkle with cheese and parsley. Bake 5 minutes more or until fish flakes easily when tested with fork. Makes 6 servings.

Cheesy Tuna and Twists

*For a heartier cheese flavor, use sharp Cheddar
instead of mozzarella.*

8 ounces corkscrew macaroni,
uncooked
2 tablespoons margarine
or butter
1 package (10 ounces) frozen
mixed vegetables, thawed
1 clove garlic, minced
1 can (10¾ ounces) Campbell's
condensed cream of
mushroom soup

¾ cup milk
1½ cups shredded mozzarella
cheese (6 ounces)
⅛ teaspoon pepper
Generous dash ground
nutmeg
1 can (6½ ounces) tuna,
drained
Chopped pimento for garnish

1. Cook macaroni according to package directions; drain.

2. Meanwhile, in 10-inch skillet over medium heat, in hot margarine,
cook mixed vegetables and garlic 2 minutes, stirring often.

3. Add soup to skillet; stir until smooth. Gradually stir in milk. Add
cheese, pepper and nutmeg; heat until cheese melts, stirring
occasionally.

4. Stir in tuna and cooked macaroni. Heat through. Garnish with
pimento. Makes 6 cups or 4 servings.

Broccoli Fish Chowder

Use haddock, halibut or cod in this vegetable chowder.

3 tablespoons margarine
or butter
1 cup sliced celery
1 cup chopped onions
2 cloves garlic, minced
¼ cup Chablis or other dry
white wine
2 cans (10¾ ounces *each*)
Campbell's condensed
cream of broccoli soup

2 cups milk
1 pound firm white fish fillets,
cut into 1-inch pieces
2 tablespoons diced pimento
Generous dash ground
red pepper

1. In 3-quart saucepan over medium heat, in hot margarine, cook
celery, onions and garlic until tender, stirring often.

2. Add wine; cook 2 minutes. Add soup; stir until smooth. Gradually
stir in milk. Add fish, pimento and red pepper. Heat to boiling.
Reduce heat to low. Cover; simmer 5 minutes or until fish flakes
easily when tested with fork. Makes 3½ cups or 4 servings.

Curried Chicken-Vegetable Chowder

Serve with classic oyster crackers or pass a basket of seasoned pita chips or bagel chips. Pictured opposite.

1 can (10¾ ounces) Campbell's condensed cream of chicken soup
1 can (10½ ounces) Campbell's condensed chicken broth
2 cups water
½ teaspoon curry powder
⅛ teaspoon dried thyme leaves, crushed

⅛ teaspoon pepper
2 cups cubed peeled potatoes (3 medium)
2 cups cubed cooked chicken
1 cup broccoli flowerets
1 cup sliced fresh mushrooms
½ cup sweet red pepper cut in strips

1. In 3-quart saucepan, stir soup until smooth. Gradually stir in broth, water, curry, thyme and pepper. Over medium heat, heat to boiling. Add potatoes. Boil 10 minutes.

2. Add remaining ingredients. Reduce heat to low. Cover; simmer 5 minutes or until vegetables are tender. Makes 8 cups or 6 servings.

Lemon-Broccoli Chicken   6 OR LESS

This easy skillet dish is one of Campbell's most popular recipes according to a recent consumer survey.

1 lemon
1 tablespoon vegetable oil
2 whole chicken breasts, split, skinned and boned (about 1 pound boneless)

1 can (10¾ ounces) Campbell's condensed cream of broccoli or cream of mushroom soup
¼ cup milk
⅛ teaspoon pepper

1. Cut 4 thin slices of lemon; set aside. Squeeze 2 teaspoons juice from remaining lemon; set aside.

2. In 10-inch skillet over medium heat, in hot oil, cook chicken 10 minutes or until browned on both sides. Spoon off fat.

3. Meanwhile, in small bowl, combine soup and milk; stir in reserved lemon juice and pepper. Pour over chicken; top each chicken piece with lemon slice.

4. Reduce heat to low. Cover; simmer 5 minutes or until chicken is tender and juices run clear, stirring occasionally. Makes 4 servings.

Curried Chicken-Vegetable Chowder

Chicken with Julienne Vegetables 🍵

Look for packaged spinach noodle nests at your supermarket. Or make your own by twirling cooked pasta with fork before serving. Pictured opposite.

1 can (10¾ ounces) Campbell's condensed creamy chicken mushroom soup
¼ cup milk
¼ teaspoon dried thyme leaves, crushed
2 whole chicken breasts, split, skinned and boned (about 1 pound boneless)

2 cups carrots cut in 2-inch julienne strips
2 cups zucchini cut in 2-inch julienne strips
Fresh thyme leaves for garnish

1. In 10-inch skillet, combine soup, milk and dried thyme. Over medium heat, heat to boiling. Add chicken and carrots. Reduce heat to low. Cover; simmer 10 minutes, stirring occasionally.

2. Add zucchini. Cover; cook 5 minutes or until chicken is tender and juices run clear. Garnish with fresh thyme. Makes 4 servings.

Broccoli Chicken Dijon

Fresh broccoli flowerets can be used instead of frozen— just steam until tender-crisp.

2 cups frozen cut broccoli (8 ounces)
2 tablespoons vegetable oil
1 pound boneless chicken breasts, cut into 2- by 1-inch strips
1 can (10¾ ounces) Campbell's condensed cream of broccoli soup

½ soup can milk
½ cup shredded Swiss cheese (2 ounces)
2 tablespoons Dijon-style mustard
2 tablespoons chopped pimento
Hot cooked rice

1. Prepare broccoli according to package directions; drain.

2. Meanwhile, in 10-inch skillet over medium-high heat, in hot oil, stir-fry chicken until browned.

3. Stir in soup, milk, cheese, mustard, pimento and cooked broccoli. Heat to boiling. Reduce heat to low. Cover; simmer 5 minutes, stirring occasionally. Serve over rice. Makes 4 cups or 4 servings.

Chicken with Julienne Vegetables

Chicken Pineapple Stir-Fry

Save time by cutting up vegetables and chicken in advance.

1 can (8 ounces) pineapple chunks
1 can (10½ ounces) Campbell's condensed chicken broth
2 tablespoons cornstarch
2 tablespoons soy sauce
¼ teaspoon ground ginger

2 tablespoons vegetable oil
2 cups broccoli flowerets
½ cup diagonally sliced carrot
2 cups cubed cooked chicken or turkey
Hot cooked rice

1. Drain pineapple, reserving juice. In small bowl, combine reserved juice, broth, cornstarch, soy sauce and ginger; set aside.

2. In 10-inch skillet over high heat, in hot oil, stir-fry broccoli and carrot until tender-crisp.

3. Stir in chicken and broth mixture. Reduce heat to medium-high. Cook until mixture boils and thickens, stirring often. Add pineapple; heat through. Serve over rice. Serve with additional *soy sauce*, if desired. Makes 4½ cups or 4 servings.

> *If you cook one pound boneless chicken breasts in advance, you'll be able to prepare any dish that calls for cubed cooked chicken. Each pound of chicken yields 2 cups cubed chicken.*

Chicken in Spicy Peanut Sauce

3 whole chicken breasts, split, skinned and boned (about 1½ pounds boneless)
2 tablespoons vegetable oil
1 can (10¾ ounces) Campbell's condensed cream of chicken soup

3 tablespoons chunky peanut butter
⅔ cup water
2 green onions, sliced
1 teaspoon chili powder
⅛ teaspoon ground red pepper

1. Place chicken breasts between 2 sheets of plastic wrap. With meat mallet or rolling pin, pound to ¼-inch thickness.

2. In 10-inch skillet over medium heat, in hot oil, cook chicken 10 minutes or until browned on both sides. Remove chicken from skillet. Spoon off fat.

3. Add soup, peanut butter, water, green onions, chili powder and red pepper to skillet; stir until smooth. Over medium heat, heat to boiling. Reduce heat to low. Return chicken to skillet. Cover; simmer 5 minutes or until chicken is tender and juices run clear. Makes 6 servings.

Mandarin Chicken

1 can (10½ ounces) Campbell's
   condensed chicken broth,
   divided
2 tablespoons cornstarch
¼ cup vinegar
¼ cup sugar
1 tablespoon soy sauce
½ teaspoon ground ginger
1 can (8 ounces) sliced water
   chestnuts, drained

1 pound skinless, boneless
   chicken breasts, cut into
   1-inch chunks
1 small green or sweet red
   pepper, cut into strips
1 can (11 ounces) mandarin
   orange segments, drained
Hot cooked rice

1. In cup, stir together ¼ cup of the broth and the cornstarch until well blended; set aside.

2. In 10-inch skillet over medium heat, combine remaining broth, vinegar, sugar, soy sauce, ginger and water chestnuts. Heat to boiling.

3. Add chicken to skillet. Reduce heat to low. Simmer 10 minutes. Add green pepper; cook 3 minutes more or until chicken is tender and juices run clear.

4. Stir in cornstarch mixture. Cook over medium heat until mixture boils and thickens, stirring constantly. Gently stir in oranges. Serve over rice. Makes 4 cups or 4 servings.

Souper Chicken Tetrazzini

8 ounces spaghetti, uncooked
2 tablespoons margarine
   or butter
2 cups sliced fresh mushrooms
1 small onion, chopped
2 cans (10¾ ounces) Campbell's
   condensed cream of
   chicken soup

1 soup can milk
2 tablespoons dry sherry
2 cups cubed cooked chicken
⅓ cup grated Parmesan cheese
¼ cup chopped fresh parsley

1. Cook spaghetti according to package directions; drain.

2. Meanwhile, in 2-quart saucepan over medium heat, in hot margarine, cook mushrooms and onion until tender, stirring occasionally. Stir in soup, milk and sherry; heat through.

3. Return cooked spaghetti to cooking pot. Add soup mixture, chicken, Parmesan and parsley. Toss lightly until spaghetti is coated. Over medium heat, heat through. Serve with additional *Parmesan*, if desired. Makes 6 cups or 4 servings.

Garden-Style Vegetable Bisque

Serve with hot garlic bread and a tossed green salad.
Pictured opposite.

2 tablespoons margarine
   or butter
1 small zucchini, halved
   lengthwise and cut into
   ½-inch slices
2 medium carrots, cut into
   2-inch julienne strips
½ cup thinly sliced celery
1 clove garlic, minced
½ teaspoon dried oregano
   leaves, crushed

1 can (11 ounces) Campbell's
   condensed Cheddar cheese
   soup/sauce
1 can (10¾ ounces) Campbell's
   condensed cream of
   potato soup
1 soup can milk
1 soup can water
1½ cups chopped cooked chicken
1 medium tomato, seeded and
   chopped

1. In 3-quart saucepan over medium heat, in hot margarine, cook zucchini, carrots, celery, garlic and oregano 10 minutes or until vegetables are tender, stirring occasionally.

2. Add soups, milk and water; stir until smooth. Stir in chicken and tomato. Cover; heat through, stirring occasionally. Makes 7½ cups or 5 servings.

Easy Creole Soup   *EXTRA EASY*

This Southern-style soup uses the family-sized 26-ounce can of condensed tomato soup. For 2 servings, follow the directions below using a 10¾-ounce can of tomato soup.

1 can (26 ounces) Campbell's
   condensed tomato soup
1 soup can water
1 large green pepper, chopped
1 medium onion, chopped

1 cup cooked rice
1 cup coarsely chopped cooked
   shrimp
½ teaspoon Louisiana-style
   hot sauce

In 2½-quart saucepan, combine all ingredients. Over medium heat, heat through. Makes 7⅔ cups or 6 servings.

Creole Soup For Two: In 1½-quart saucepan, combine 1 can (10¾ ounces) Campbell's condensed tomato soup and 1 soup can water. Halve remaining ingredients. Proceed as directed above. Makes 3½ cups or 2 servings.

Garden-Style Vegetable Bisque

eeseburger Pizza

This giant open-face cheeseburger tastes good topped with any of your favorite burger fixings. Pictured opposite.

2 packages (7½ ounces *each*) refrigerated biscuits

¾ pound ground beef

½ cup chopped onion

1 can (11 ounces) Campbell's condensed Cheddar cheese soup/sauce

1 can (8 ounces) tomatoes, drained, cut up

2 tablespoons sliced green onion

2 teaspoons prepared mustard

⅛ teaspoon hot pepper sauce

½ cup shredded mozzarella cheese (2 ounces)

Sliced onion, hamburger dill pickle chips, mustard and ketchup for garnish

1. Preheat oven to 400°F. Meanwhile, press biscuits into 12-inch round on greased baking sheet or 12-inch pizza pan, pinching edges of biscuits together to seal. Bake 10 minutes.

2. Meanwhile, in 10-inch skillet over medium heat, cook beef and onion until beef is browned and onion is tender, stirring to separate meat. Spoon off fat. Stir in next five ingredients. Heat through.

3. Spread beef mixture over biscuits to within ½ inch of edge. Sprinkle with cheese. Bake 5 minutes or until biscuits are golden brown. Garnish as desired. Cut into wedges. Makes 6 servings.

Meatball Mushroom Sandwiches

½ pound ground beef

½ pound Italian sausage, casing removed

¼ cup fine dry bread crumbs

1 egg, beaten

½ teaspoon dried oregano leaves, crushed

2 tablespoons vegetable oil

1 can (10¾ ounces) Campbell's condensed golden mushroom soup

½ cup water

4 long hard rolls (*each* 8 inches long), split lengthwise

1. In medium bowl, combine beef, sausage, bread crumbs, egg and oregano; mix lightly, but well. Shape into 16 (1½-inch) meatballs.

2. In 10-inch skillet over medium heat, in hot oil, cook meatballs 10 minutes or until browned on all sides. Spoon off fat.

3. Stir in soup and water. Heat to boiling. Reduce heat to low. Cover; simmer 10 minutes or until meatballs are thoroughly cooked, stirring occasionally. Spoon 4 meatballs and about ¼ cup of the sauce onto each roll. Makes 4 servings.

Cheeseburger Pizza

Piquant Pork Chops

Accompany with a fresh fruit salad sprinkled with a little lemon or lime juice.

4 boneless pork chops, cut
   ½ inch thick (about
   1 pound)
¼ teaspoon pepper
1 tablespoon vegetable oil
1 can (10½ ounces) Campbell's
   condensed chicken broth

3 tablespoons lime juice
1 tablespoon sugar
1 teaspoon Dijon-style mustard
4 teaspoons cornstarch
2 tablespoons water
   Hot cooked rice

1. Sprinkle pork chops with pepper. In 10-inch skillet over medium heat, in hot oil, cook chops until browned on both sides.

2. Stir in broth, lime juice, sugar and mustard. Heat to boiling. Reduce heat to low. Cover; simmer 10 minutes.

3. Transfer chops to platter. In cup, stir together cornstarch and water until well blended; gradually stir into skillet. Cook over high heat until mixture boils and thickens, stirring often. Serve with rice. Makes 4 servings.

Garlic Orange Beef

3 tablespoons vegetable oil,
   divided
1 pound boneless beef sirloin
   steak, thinly sliced
1 medium onion, chopped
1 clove garlic, minced
1 teaspoon orange peel cut in
   1-inch-long thin strips
1 can (10¾ ounces) Campbell's
   condensed beefy mushroom
   soup

⅓ cup water
¼ cup tomato paste
¼ cup orange juice
2 tablespoons molasses
⅛ teaspoon pepper
   Hot cooked noodles

1. In 10-inch skillet over high heat, in *2 tablespoons* hot oil, cook *half* the beef until color just changes, stirring often. Transfer beef to bowl. Repeat with remaining beef.

2. Reduce heat to medium. In remaining oil, cook onion, garlic and orange peel 3 minutes, stirring often.

3. Stir in soup, water, tomato paste, orange juice, molasses and pepper. Heat to boiling. Reduce heat to low; simmer 5 minutes. Add beef; cook 5 minutes more, stirring occasionally. Serve over noodles. Makes 3½ cups or 4 servings.

Cincinnati Chili ◇EXTRA EASY◇

1 pound ground beef
1 cup chopped green pepper
½ cup chopped onion
2 cloves garlic, minced
3 tablespoons chili powder
2 cans (10¾ ounces) Campbell's
  condensed tomato soup

1 can (15 ounces) kidney beans,
  undrained
1 tablespoon vinegar
¼ teaspoon ground cinnamon
  Hot cooked spaghetti
  Shredded Cheddar cheese
    for garnish
  Sour cream for garnish

1. In 4-quart saucepan over medium heat, cook beef, green pepper,
   onion, garlic and chili powder until beef is browned and vegetables
   are tender, stirring to separate meat. Spoon off fat.

2. Stir in soup, kidney beans, vinegar and cinnamon. Heat to boiling.
   Reduce heat to low. Simmer 15 minutes, stirring occasionally. Serve
   chili over spaghetti. Garnish with cheese and sour cream. Makes
   6 cups or 5 servings.

> *To reheat spaghetti in your microwave oven*, place in
> microwave-safe casserole. Cover with vented plastic wrap;
> microwave on HIGH 2 minutes for each 1-cup serving. Stir after
> every 2 minutes of heating.

Bean-and-Bacon Mac Skillet

3 slices bacon, cut into 1-inch
  pieces
1 small onion, chopped
3½ cups water
2 cups elbow macaroni,
  uncooked
1 can (11 ounces) Campbell's
  condensed Cheddar cheese
  soup/sauce

1 can (11 ounces) Campbell's
  condensed nacho cheese
  soup/dip
1 can (16 ounces) kidney beans,
  drained
1 medium tomato, chopped
1 cup shredded Cheddar cheese
  Chopped green onions for
  garnish

1. In 10-inch skillet over medium heat, cook bacon and onion until
   bacon is crisp, stirring occasionally.

2. Add water. Heat to boiling. Add macaroni. Cook 10 to 12 minutes or
   until macaroni is tender, stirring often.

3. In large bowl, stir soups until smooth. Add beans, tomato and
   macaroni mixture; toss lightly to mix. Return to skillet. Cover; cook
   over low heat 5 minutes or until heated through, stirring
   occasionally. Sprinkle with cheese. Garnish with green onions.
   Makes 6 cups or 6 servings.

Pineapple Beef Curry

Be creative with the condiments: chopped green and sweet red peppers, sliced green onions, canned pineapple chunks, flaked coconut, mandarin orange segments and peanuts. Pictured opposite.

1 pound ground beef
2 teaspoons curry powder
1 can (10½ ounces) Campbell's condensed beef broth
1 can (8 ounces) tomatoes, drained, cut up
1 can (8 ounces) crushed pineapple in juice, undrained

3 tablespoons tomato paste
2 tablespoons apricot preserves
4 green onions, diagonally sliced
Hot cooked rice
Assorted condiments (see suggestions above)

1. In 10-inch skillet over medium heat, cook beef until browned, stirring to separate meat. Add curry; cook 2 minutes more.

2. Stir in broth, tomatoes, pineapple, tomato paste and preserves. Heat to boiling. Reduce heat to low. Simmer 10 minutes, stirring occasionally.

3. Stir in green onions; simmer 5 minutes more or until tender, stirring occasionally. Serve over rice with assorted condiments. Makes 4 cups or 4 servings.

Southwest Mac and Beef

For extra fire, serve with hot chili peppers.

1 pound ground beef
1 medium onion, chopped
½ teaspoon ground cumin
1 can (11 ounces) Campbell's condensed Cheddar cheese soup/sauce
1 can (10½ ounces) Campbell's condensed beef broth

2 soup cans water
1 can (15 ounces) stewed tomatoes
1 can (4 ounces) chopped green chilies
½ cup elbow macaroni, uncooked

1. In 4-quart Dutch oven over medium heat, cook beef, onion and cumin until beef is browned, stirring to separate meat. Spoon off fat.

2. Add soup; stir until smooth. Stir in broth, water, tomatoes and chilies. Heat to boiling. Add macaroni. Reduce heat to low. Cook 12 minutes or until macaroni is tender, stirring occasionally. Makes 6 cups or 4 servings.

Pineapple Beef Curry

Taco Salad

Let everyone build their own salad—just assemble the ingredients in advance. Pictured opposite.

1 pound ground beef
¼ cup chopped onion
1 tablespoon chili powder
1 can (11 ounces) Campbell's condensed nacho cheese soup/dip
1 can (16 ounces) pinto beans, drained

4 cups torn mixed salad greens
Tortilla chips
Chopped fresh tomato
Sliced avocado for garnish
Sliced pitted ripe olives for garnish

1. In 10-inch skillet over medium heat, cook beef, onion and chili powder until beef is browned, stirring to separate meat. Spoon off fat.

2. Stir in soup and beans. Heat to boiling. Reduce heat to low. Simmer 5 minutes, stirring occasionally.

3. Arrange salad greens and tortilla chips on serving plate. Top with hot meat mixture. Top with tomato. Garnish as desired. Serve with additional *tortilla chips*, if desired. Makes 4 servings.

Anise Beef and Rice

2 tablespoons vegetable oil
1 pound boneless top round beef steak, thinly sliced
3 cups coarsely chopped bok choy
½ cup yellow squash cut in 2-inch julienne strips
1 can (10½ ounces) Campbell's condensed beef broth

¼ cup dry sherry
2 tablespoons soy sauce
¼ teaspoon anise seed
2 tablespoons cornstarch
½ cup water
1 cup cherry tomatoes *each* cut in half
Hot cooked rice

1. In 10-inch skillet over high heat, in hot oil, cook beef *half* at a time, until beef just changes color, stirring constantly. Transfer to bowl.

2. Add bok choy and squash to skillet. Over high heat, cook 1 minute, stirring often. Stir in broth, sherry, soy sauce and anise. Heat to boiling.

3. Meanwhile, in cup, stir together cornstarch and water until well blended; gradually stir into broth mixture. Cook until mixture boils and thickens, stirring often. Add cooked beef and cherry tomatoes. Cook 2 minutes or until heated through, stirring often. Serve over rice. Makes 5 cups or 4 servings.

Taco Salad

Cheesy Mushroom Frittata

Serve with fresh fruit or mini croissants. Pictured opposite.

1 can (10¾ ounces) Campbell's
condensed cream of
mushroom soup
6 eggs, slightly beaten
1½ cups shredded mozzarella
cheese (6 ounces), divided
¼ teaspoon dried basil leaves,
crushed
⅛ teaspoon pepper

2 tablespoons margarine
or butter
1 cup sliced fresh mushrooms
1 medium onion, chopped
Chopped fresh parsley for
garnish
Tomato wedges for garnish
Fresh basil leaves for garnish

1. In medium bowl with wire whisk, beat soup until smooth. Gradually
blend in eggs, *1 cup* of the cheese, the basil and pepper.

2. In 10-inch *oven-safe* omelet pan or skillet over medium heat, in hot
margarine, cook mushrooms and onion until mushrooms are tender
and liquid is evaporated, stirring occasionally.

3. Pour mixture into skillet. Reduce heat to low. Cook 6 minutes or
until eggs are set 1 inch from edge. *Do not stir.* Remove from heat.

4. Broil 6 inches from heat 5 minutes or until frittata is puffy and
lightly browned. Top with remaining cheese. Cover; let stand
2 minutes or until cheese melts. Garnish with parsley, tomato
wedges and fresh basil. Makes 5 servings.

Bavarian Kielbasa with Noodles   *EXTRA EASY*

6 ounces egg noodles, uncooked
¾ pound smoked kielbasa, cut up
1 medium onion, sliced
1 can (10¾ ounces) Campbell's
condensed cream of
mushroom soup

1 soup can milk
1½ cups frozen cut green beans
⅛ teaspoon pepper
Spicy brown mustard
(optional)

1. Cook noodles according to package directions; drain. Meanwhile, in
10-inch skillet over medium heat, cook kielbasa and onion until
browned, stirring often. Spoon off fat.

2. Add soup; stir until smooth. Gradually stir in milk. Add beans and
pepper. Heat to boiling. Reduce heat to low. Cover; simmer
5 minutes or until beans are tender, stirring occasionally.

3. Stir cooked noodles into skillet. Heat 2 minutes, stirring often. Serve
with mustard, if desired. Makes 6 cups or 4 servings.

Cheesy Mushroom Frittata

Fiesta Eggs 〰〰 6 OR LESS

*For a Mexican flair, omit the potatoes and wrap eggs
in warmed corn tortillas.*

4 frozen shredded potato patties
1 can (11 ounces) Campbell's
  condensed nacho cheese
  soup/dip, divided
8 eggs, slightly beaten
2 tablespoons milk
2 tablespoons margarine
  or butter

1 cup shredded Monterey Jack
  cheese (4 ounces)
Sliced green onions for
  garnish
Chopped sweet red pepper
  for garnish

1. Prepare potato patties according to package directions.

2. Meanwhile, in medium bowl, stir ½ *can* of the soup until smooth.
   Gradually blend in eggs.

3. For sauce: In 1-quart saucepan, combine remaining soup and milk.
   Over medium heat, heat through, stirring constantly. Cover;
   keep warm.

4. In 10-inch skillet over medium heat, in hot margarine, cook egg
   mixture. As eggs begin to set, stir lightly so uncooked egg flows to
   bottom. Cook until eggs are set but still moist.

5. Sprinkle ¼ *cup* of the cheese over each cooked potato patty. Bake
   until cheese melts.

6. Arrange eggs on top of each potato patty; spoon about
   2 *tablespoons* of the sauce over each. Garnish with green onions
   and red pepper. Makes 4 servings.

To microwave: Omit margarine. Prepare potato patties as directed in
step 1. Meanwhile, in 3-quart microwave-safe casserole, stir ½ *can* of
the soup until smooth. Gradually blend in eggs. Cover with lid;
microwave on HIGH 6½ minutes or until eggs are nearly set, stirring
3 times during cooking. Let stand, covered, 2 minutes. For sauce: In
1-quart casserole, stir remaining soup until smooth. Stir in milk. Cover
with lid; microwave on HIGH 2 minutes or until hot, stirring once
during cooking. Serve as directed in step 6.

Sausage Skillet Dinner

To save time, purchase prepared coleslaw at a deli or supermarket to complete this skillet meal.

1 pound smoked kielbasa, cut
  into $1/2$-inch slices
1 can ($10^1/2$ ounces) Campbell's
  condensed French onion
  soup
$1/4$ cup water
2 cups frozen mixed vegetables

1 can (8 ounces) tomatoes,
  undrained, cut up
$1/8$ teaspoon pepper
$1^1/2$ cups quick-cooking rice,
  uncooked
Chopped fresh parsley for
  garnish

1. In 10-inch skillet over medium heat, cook sausage until browned, stirring often. Spoon off fat.

2. Add soup, water, vegetables, tomatoes and pepper. Heat to boiling. Reduce heat to low. Simmer 2 minutes or until vegetables are tender. Stir in rice. Remove from heat. Cover; let stand 5 minutes or until most of the liquid is absorbed. Fluff rice with fork before serving. Garnish with parsley. Makes 6 cups or 4 servings.

Hearty Sausage 'n' Cabbage Soup

Serve with slices of crusty rye or pumpernickel bread.

$1/2$ pound ground beef
$1/2$ pound Italian sausage, casing
  removed
2 cups coarsely chopped
  cabbage
$1/2$ cup finely chopped carrot
1 can ($10^3/4$ ounces) Campbell's
  condensed golden
  mushroom soup

1 can ($10^1/2$ ounces) Campbell's
  condensed French onion
  soup
2 soup cans water
1 can (16 ounces) whole
  potatoes, drained, cut into
  1-inch pieces

1. In 5-quart Dutch oven over high heat, cook beef and sausage until browned, stirring to separate meat.

2. Add cabbage and carrot. Cook 5 minutes, stirring often. Spoon off fat.

3. Stir in soups, water and potatoes. Heat to boiling. Reduce heat to low. Cover; simmer 10 minutes or until carrots are tender. Makes about 7 cups or 5 servings.

Turkey-Vegetable Pot Pie

Toss together a garden salad while this bakes. For a different touch, add sunflower seeds, sliced red onions and snipped dried apricots to the salad greens. Pictured opposite.

1 package (16 ounces) frozen mixed vegetables (broccoli, cauliflower and carrots)
2 tablespoons margarine or butter
$1/2$ cup chopped onion
$1/2$ cup sliced celery
$1/2$ teaspoon dried thyme leaves, crushed
1 can ($10^3/4$ ounces) Campbell's condensed cream of broccoli soup
1 can ($10^3/4$ ounces) Campbell's condensed cream of chicken soup
1 cup milk
3 cups diced cooked turkey or chicken
$1/4$ teaspoon pepper
1 package (8 ounces) refrigerated crescent rolls

1. Preheat oven to 375°F. Cook vegetables according to package directions; drain.

2. Meanwhile, in 2-quart saucepan over medium heat, in hot margarine, cook onion, celery and thyme until onion is tender, stirring occasionally. Add soups and milk; stir until smooth.

3. In 12- by 8-inch baking dish, combine turkey, cooked vegetables and pepper. Add soup mixture, stirring gently to mix.

4. Unroll crescent rolls without separating pieces. Firmly press perforations to seal. Cut dough lengthwise into 8 strips, about $3/4$ inch wide. Arrange dough strips over chicken mixture to form a lattice, cutting strips as necessary to fit. Press ends of strips to baking dish.

5. Bake 30 minutes or until golden brown. Cover edges with foil after 20 minutes of baking if pastry browns too quickly. Makes 6 servings.

Turkey-Vegetable Pot Pie

Chicken Enchiladas

Corn tortillas can be substituted for the flour ones.

1 can (10¾ ounces) Campbell's
   condensed cream of celery
   soup
½ cup sour cream
2 tablespoons margarine
   or butter
½ cup chopped onion

1 teaspoon chili powder
2 cups diced cooked chicken
1 can (4 ounces) chopped
   green chilies
8 flour tortillas (7-inch)
1 cup shredded Monterey Jack
   cheese (4 ounces)

1. Preheat oven to 375°F. In small bowl, stir together soup and sour cream until smooth; set aside.

2. In 2-quart saucepan over medium heat, in hot margarine, cook onion and chili powder until onion is tender, stirring often. Stir in chicken, chilies and *2 tablespoons* of the soup mixture. Remove from heat.

3. To make enchiladas: Along center of each tortilla, spread about ¼ *cup* of the chicken mixture; fold sides over filling and place seam-side down in greased 12- by 8-inch baking dish.

4. Spread remaining soup mixture over enchiladas. Cover with foil; bake 15 minutes. Sprinkle with cheese. Bake, uncovered, 5 minutes more or until cheese melts. Makes 4 servings.

Classic Glorified Chicken

A Campbell recipe collection favorite because it's so easy to prepare and uses only three ingredients!

2½- to 3-pound broiler-fryer
   chicken, cut up
1 tablespoon margarine or
   butter, melted

1 can (10¾ ounces) Campbell's
   condensed cream of
   chicken, cream of celery,
   cream of mushroom, golden
   mushroom or cream of
   broccoli soup
Chopped fresh parsley for
   garnish

1. Preheat oven to 375°F. Meanwhile, in 12- by 8-inch baking dish, arrange chicken skin-side up. Drizzle with margarine. Bake 40 minutes.

2. Spoon soup over chicken. Bake 20 minutes more or until chicken is tender and juices run clear. Transfer chicken to platter. Stir sauce; spoon sauce over chicken. Garnish with parsley. Makes 4 servings.

Country-Style Smothered Chicken

2 slices bacon
2½-to 3-pound broiler-fryer
   chicken, cut up
1 can (10¾ ounces) Campbell's
   condensed cream of
   mushroom soup

1 clove garlic, minced
1 teaspoon dried basil leaves,
   crushed
1 medium onion, sliced
   Hot cooked rice

1. In 10-inch skillet over medium heat, cook bacon until crisp. Transfer to paper towels to drain, reserving drippings in pan. Crumble bacon; set aside.

2. Over medium heat, in hot drippings, cook chicken 10 minutes or until browned on all sides. Spoon off fat.

3. Add soup, garlic and basil; stir until smooth. Heat to boiling. Reduce heat to low. Cover; simmer 20 minutes.

4. Add onion. Cover; simmer 15 minutes more or until chicken is tender and juices run clear, stirring occasionally. Sprinkle with crumbled bacon. Serve with rice. Makes 6 servings.

For crisp bacon in a hurry, microwave it. One slice of bacon cooks in about one minute.

Shortcut Brunswick Stew

2 slices bacon
½ cup chopped onion
1 can (10¾ ounces) Campbell's
   condensed tomato soup
1 soup can water
1 teaspoon Worcestershire
   sauce

Generous dash pepper
1 package (10 ounces) frozen
   Fordhook lima beans
1 package (10 ounces) frozen
   whole kernel corn
2 cups cubed cooked chicken

1. In 3-quart saucepan over low heat, cook bacon until crisp. Transfer to paper towels to drain, reserving *1 tablespoon* drippings in pan. Crumble bacon; set aside.

2. Over medium heat, in hot drippings, cook onion until tender, stirring occasionally.

3. Stir in soup, water, Worcestershire and pepper. Heat to boiling. Add lima beans and corn. Return to boiling. Stir to separate vegetables. Reduce heat to low. Cover; simmer 20 minutes.

4. Stir in chicken and cooked bacon; heat through. Makes about 6 cups or 4 servings.

Easy Paella

This easy and colorful skillet meal is sure to be a hit. Serve with a chilled marinated cucumber salad and French bread. Pictured opposite and on back cover.

1 can (6$\frac{1}{2}$ ounces) chopped clams
2 tablespoons vegetable oil
8 chicken thighs (about 2$\frac{1}{2}$ pounds)
1 large onion, chopped
1$\frac{1}{2}$ cups regular rice, uncooked
2 cloves garlic, minced

2 cans (10$\frac{1}{2}$ ounces *each*) Campbell's condensed chicken broth
$\frac{1}{2}$ teaspoon ground turmeric
$\frac{1}{2}$ teaspoon pepper
1 package (10 ounces) frozen peas
$\frac{1}{2}$ pound medium shrimp, shelled and deveined
Lemon wedges

1. Drain clams, reserving liquid. Add enough water to clam liquid to make 1$\frac{1}{4}$ cups; set aside.

2. In 6-quart Dutch oven over medium-high heat, in hot oil, cook chicken 10 minutes or until browned on all sides. Remove chicken; set aside.

3. Reduce heat to medium. In hot drippings, cook onion, rice and garlic until rice is lightly browned, stirring often. Add reserved clam liquid, broth, turmeric, pepper and chicken. Heat to boiling. Reduce heat to low. Cover; simmer 30 minutes or until chicken is tender and juices run clear.

4. Stir in clams, peas and shrimp. Cover; cook 5 minutes or until shrimp turn pink and opaque. Serve with lemon. Makes 8 servings.

Chicken Stuffing Bake   *EXTRA EASY*

1 can (10$\frac{3}{4}$ ounces) Campbell's condensed cream of mushroom soup
1 cup milk
1 package (7 ounces) herb-seasoned stuffing mix

2 cups cubed cooked chicken
2 cups cooked broccoli flowerets
2 stalks celery, finely chopped
1$\frac{1}{2}$ cups shredded Swiss cheese (6 ounces), divided

1. Preheat oven to 375°F. Meanwhile, in large bowl, stir soup until smooth. Gradually stir in milk. Add stuffing mix, chicken, broccoli, celery and *1 cup* of the cheese. Spread mixture in greased 12- by 8-inch baking dish.

2. Bake 20 minutes. Top with remaining cheese; bake until cheese melts. Makes 6 servings.

Easy Paella

try Herbed Chicken

like, substitute sliced carrots and quartered cooking onions for the same delicious results. You can also serve with steamed red potatoes as shown in photo. Pictured opposite.

2 tablespoons vegetable oil
2½- to 3-pound broiler-fryer
    chicken, cut up
2 cans (10¾ ounces *each*)
    Campbell's condensed
    creamy chicken mushroom
    soup
½ cup Chablis or other dry
    white wine

2 tablespoons chopped
    fresh parsley
½ teaspoon dried thyme leaves,
    crushed
¼ teaspoon dried rosemary
    leaves, crushed
½ pound whole baby carrots
8 small whole white onions
    Hot cooked red potatoes
    (optional)

1. In 4-quart Dutch oven over medium-high heat, in hot oil, cook chicken 10 minutes or until browned on all sides. Remove chicken; set aside. Spoon off fat.

2. Add next five ingredients. Return chicken to Dutch oven. Heat to boiling. Reduce heat to low. Cover; simmer 15 minutes. Add carrots and onions. Simmer 20 minutes or until chicken is tender and juices run clear. Serve with potatoes, if desired. Makes 4 servings.

Chicken-Broccoli-Rice Skillet

2 tablespoons margarine or
    butter
¾ cup finely chopped carrots
¼ cup chopped green onions
1 pound skinless, boneless
    chicken breasts, cut into
    thin strips

1 can (10¾ ounces) Campbell's
    condensed cream of
    broccoli soup
1 cup milk
⅛ teaspoon pepper
1¼ cups quick-cooking rice,
    uncooked
    Chopped green onions
    for garnish

1. In 10-inch skillet over medium heat, in hot margarine, cook carrots and green onions until tender, stirring occasionally. Push to one side. Add chicken, *half* at a time, cooking until browned on all sides, stirring frequently. Remove chicken as it browns. Return chicken to skillet. Stir in soup, milk and pepper. Heat to boiling. Reduce heat to low. Cover; simmer 10 minutes, stirring occasionally.

2. Stir in rice. Remove from heat. Cover; let stand 5 minutes or until most of liquid is absorbed. Fluff with fork before serving. Garnish with green onions. Makes about 5½ cups or 4 servings.

Country Herbed Chicken

Chicken-Broccoli Cordon Bleu

For Chicken Cordon Bleu, substitute cream of chicken soup for the broccoli soup. Pictured opposite.

2 whole chicken breasts, split, skinned and boned (about 1 pound boneless)

4 thin slices (1 ounce *each*) fully cooked ham

4 thin slices (1 ounce *each*) Swiss cheese

2 tablespoons vegetable oil

1 can (10¾ ounces) Campbell's condensed cream of broccoli soup

⅓ cup milk

¼ cup sliced green onions

⅛ teaspoon dried thyme leaves, crushed

Chopped fresh parsley for garnish

1. Place chicken between 2 pieces of plastic wrap. With meat mallet or rolling pin, pound chicken to ¼-inch thickness. Place a ham slice and cheese slice on *each* breast half. Roll up chicken from narrow end, jelly-roll fashion. Tuck in ham and cheese if necessary; secure with wooden toothpicks.

2. In 10-inch skillet over medium heat, in hot oil, cook chicken 10 minutes or until browned on all sides. Spoon off fat.

3. Stir in soup, milk, green onions and thyme. Heat to boiling. Reduce heat to low. Cover; simmer 10 minutes or until chicken is tender and juices run clear. Garnish with parsley. Makes 4 servings.

To microwave: Omit oil. Prepare chicken rolls as directed in step 1. Place chicken seam-side down in 12- by 8-inch microwave-safe baking dish. Cover with vented plastic wrap; microwave on HIGH 5 minutes. In small bowl, combine soup, milk, green onions and thyme. Pour over chicken. Cover; microwave on HIGH 10 minutes or until chicken is tender and juices run clear, rotating dish halfway through cooking. Let stand, covered, 5 minutes. Garnish as directed in step 3.

> *To save time at the last minute, prepare greens for salads in advance.* Rinse greens with cold water and drain. Pat dry with paper towels or spin in salad spinner. Then refrigerate in sealed plastic bag.

Chicken-Broccoli Cordon Bleu

Tamale Pie

1 pound ground beef
2 teaspoons chili powder
1 can (10³/₄ ounces) Campbell's
   condensed tomato soup
1 cup coarsely chopped green
   pepper

1 cup whole kernel corn
¹/₂ cup salsa
¹/₄ cup water
1 package (8¹/₂ to 12 ounces)
   corn muffin mix

1. Preheat oven to 400°F.

2. In 10-inch skillet over medium heat, cook beef and chili powder
   until beef is browned, stirring to separate meat. Spoon off fat.

3. Stir in soup, green pepper, corn, salsa and water. Heat to boiling.
   Reduce heat to low. Cover; simmer 5 minutes. Pour into 2-quart
   casserole. Prepare corn muffin mix according to package directions;
   spoon evenly over soup mixture.

4. Bake 25 minutes or until a wooden toothpick inserted in center
   of muffin mixture comes out clean. Makes 6 servings.

> ***Save cleanup time**—line baking dishes with heavy-duty
> aluminum foil.*

Macaroni Ratatouille Soup

1 pound sweet Italian sausage,
   casing removed
1 medium onion, chopped
2 cloves garlic, minced
¹/₂ teaspoon dried oregano leaves,
   crushed
1 can (10³/₄ ounces) Campbell's
   condensed tomato soup
1 can (10¹/₂ ounces) Campbell's
   condensed beef broth
1 can (8 ounces) tomatoes,
   undrained, cut up

2 cups water
1 pound eggplant, cut into
   ¹/₂-inch pieces
¹/₂ teaspoon pepper
¹/₂ cup elbow macaroni,
   uncooked
Chopped fresh parsley
   for garnish
Grated Parmesan cheese
   for garnish

1. In 5-quart Dutch oven over medium heat, cook sausage, onion,
   garlic and oregano until sausage is browned, stirring to separate
   sausage. Spoon off fat.

2. Stir in soup, broth, tomatoes, water, eggplant and pepper. Heat
   to boiling. Reduce heat to low. Cover; simmer 15 minutes.

3. Stir in macaroni; cook 10 minutes more or until macaroni is tender,
   stirring occasionally. Garnish with parsley and Parmesan. Makes
   7 cups or 5 servings.

Ham Barley Soup

A hearty meal when accompanied with garlic bread or breadsticks.

3 tablespoons margarine
    or butter
1 cup sliced fresh mushrooms
1/2 cup chopped onion
1/4 teaspoon dried thyme leaves,
    crushed
2/3 cup regular pearl barley
1 can (10 1/2 ounces) Campbell's
    condensed chicken broth

1 can (10 1/2 ounces) Campbell's
    condensed beef broth
1 1/2 cups water
1/4 teaspoon pepper
1 1/2 cups milk
1/4 pound fully cooked ham, cut
    into 1 1/2-inch julienne strips
    (1 cup)
1 cup frozen peas

1. In 4-quart saucepan over medium heat, in hot margarine, cook mushrooms, onion and thyme 3 minutes, stirring occasionally. Add barley; cook 2 minutes or until golden, stirring often.

2. Add broths, water and pepper. Cover; heat to boiling. Reduce heat to low. Simmer 40 minutes.

3. Stir in milk, ham and peas. Cook 5 minutes more or until barley is tender. Makes 6 1/2 cups or 4 servings.

Sausage Stuffing Broccoli Bake

1 package (10 ounces) frozen
    chopped broccoli
1/2 pound bulk pork sausage
3 cups plain croutons
2 cups shredded sharp Cheddar
    or Swiss cheese (8 ounces)

1 can (10 3/4 ounces) Campbell's
    condensed cream of
    broccoli soup
4 eggs
1 soup can milk

1. Preheat oven to 400°F. Cook broccoli according to package directions; drain.

2. Meanwhile, in 10-inch skillet over medium heat, cook sausage until browned, stirring to separate meat. Spoon off fat.

3. In large bowl, combine cooked sausage, cooked broccoli, croutons and cheese; toss lightly to mix. Arrange mixture evenly in greased 12- by 8-inch baking dish.

4. In same bowl, stir soup until smooth. Beat in eggs and milk. Pour over sausage mixture, covering all ingredients. Bake 30 minutes or until set in center. Let stand 10 minutes before serving. Cut into squares to serve. Makes 9 servings.

Rely on your microwave oven to thaw frozen vegetables in minutes for use in a recipe—use the defrost cycle.

Nacho Pork Chili

Serve with hot cornbread sticks and whipped honey butter.
Pictured opposite.

2 tablespoons vegetable oil
1 pound boneless pork shoulder
   or loin roast, cut into
   ³/₄-inch pieces
1 clove garlic, minced
1 tablespoon chili powder
1 teaspoon ground cumin
1 can (11 ounces) Campbell's
   condensed nacho cheese
   soup/dip

1 cup beer
1 can (8 ounces) tomatoes,
   undrained, cut up
1 can (16 ounces) white or red
   kidney beans, drained
Hot cooked rice
Sour cream for garnish
Chopped green onions for
   garnish

1. In 3-quart saucepan over medium heat, in hot oil, cook pork *half* at a time, until browned on all sides, stirring occasionally. Remove pork as it browns. Return pork to saucepan. Add garlic, chili powder and cumin. Cook 5 minutes, stirring occasionally.

2. Stir in soup, beer and tomatoes. Heat to boiling. Reduce heat to low. Cover; simmer 40 minutes or until pork is tender and no pink remains. Add beans. Heat through. Serve chili over rice. Garnish with sour cream and green onions. Makes 4 cups or 4 servings.

German-Style Pork Stew

2 tablespoons vegetable oil
1 pound boneless pork shoulder
   roast, cut into
   ³/₄-inch pieces
2 cans (10³/₄ ounces *each*)
   Campbell's condensed
   cream of celery soup
³/₄ cup apple juice
¹/₂ teaspoon pepper

¹/₂ teaspoon caraway seed
2 medium red potatoes, cut into
   1-inch chunks
¹/₂ cup water
3 cups coarsely chopped
   cabbage
3 medium carrots, diagonally
   sliced
¹/₂ cup milk

1. In 4-quart saucepan over medium heat, in hot oil, cook pork *half* at a time, until browned on all sides, stirring occasionally. Remove pork as it browns.

2. Return pork to saucepan. Stir in soup, juice, pepper and caraway seed. Cover; heat to boiling. Reduce heat to low. Cook 10 minutes, stirring occasionally. Add potatoes and water. Cover; cook 10 minutes. Add cabbage and carrots. Cover; cook 15 minutes or until vegetables are tender. Stir in milk; heat through. Makes 8 cups or 6 servings.

Nacho Pork Chili

Winter Lamb Stew

Use beef stew meat instead of lamb if your family prefers. Just increase the cooking time about 20 minutes. Pictured opposite.

1 tablespoon vegetable oil
1 pound boneless lamb shoulder roast, cut into ³/₄-inch pieces
¹/₂ cup coarsely chopped onion
1 teaspoon paprika
1 can (10³/₄ ounces) Campbell's condensed beefy mushroom soup
1 can (8 ounces) tomatoes, undrained, cut up

1 soup can water
1 pound butternut or acorn squash, peeled, seeded and cut into ¹/₂-inch pieces (about 2 cups)
1 cup whole kernel corn
¹/₈ teaspoon pepper
2 tablespoons chopped fresh parsley

1. In 4-quart saucepan over medium heat, in hot oil, cook lamb *half* at a time, until browned, stirring often. Remove lamb as it browns.

2. In same saucepan over medium heat, cook onion and paprika 2 minutes, stirring occasionally. Stir in soup, tomatoes and water. Return lamb to saucepan. Heat to boiling. Reduce heat to low. Cover; simmer 25 minutes.

3. Add squash, corn and pepper. Cover; cook 15 minutes more or until lamb and vegetables are tender. Stir in parsley. Makes 4 servings.

Zesty Spinach Meat Loaves

1 can (11 ounces) Campbell's condensed zesty tomato soup, divided
2 pounds ground beef
1 package (10 ounces) frozen chopped spinach, thawed and well drained

¹/₂ cup fine dry bread crumbs
¹/₂ cup grated Parmesan cheese
¹/₂ cup finely chopped onion
2 eggs, beaten
1 tablespoon Worcestershire sauce

1. Preheat oven to 350°F. Meanwhile, in large bowl, thoroughly mix ¹/₂ *cup* of the soup with the remaining ingredients. In 13- by 9-inch baking pan, firmly shape meat mixture into two 4- by 2-inch loaves.

2. Bake 45 minutes or until done. Spoon off *2 tablespoons* of the drippings; reserve.

3. In 1-quart saucepan over medium heat, heat remaining soup and the reserved drippings to boiling, stirring occasionally. Spoon sauce over meat loaves. Makes 8 servings.

Winter Lamb Stew

Ziti Casserole

Most any combination of cooked vegetables can be used. It's a terrific way to use leftovers, too.

8 ounces ziti or mostaccioli macaroni, uncooked

2 cups frozen mixed vegetables (zucchini, green beans, carrots)

1 pound ground beef

2 cans (10¾ ounces *each*) Campbell's condensed golden mushroom soup

1 can (8 ounces) tomatoes, undrained, cut up

1 teaspoon dried basil leaves, crushed

¼ teaspoon pepper

⅛ teaspoon garlic powder

1 cup shredded sharp American process cheese (4 ounces)

1. Preheat oven to 400°F. Cook ziti and mixed vegetables according to package directions for *each*; drain. Return cooked ziti and vegetables to cooking pot used to cook ziti.

2. Meanwhile, in 10-inch skillet over medium heat, cook beef until browned, stirring to separate meat. Spoon off fat.

3. Stir in soup, tomatoes, basil, pepper and garlic. Heat through. Add soup mixture to ziti mixture; mix well. Spoon into greased 12- by 8-inch baking dish. Cover with foil; bake 15 minutes.

4. Uncover; sprinkle with cheese. Bake 5 minutes more or until cheese melts. Makes 7½ cups or 6 servings.

Calico Tuna-Rice Bake
6 OR LESS

Turn to this versatile casserole when time is short. Substitute 1 can (7½ ounces) salmon or 1½ cups cubed, cooked chicken for the tuna, if you like.

⅔ cup regular rice, uncooked

1 can (10¾ ounces) Campbell's condensed cream of celery soup

½ cup milk

1 can (6½ ounces) tuna, drained and flaked

1 cup frozen peas and carrots, thawed

1. Preheat oven to 400°F. Cook rice according to package directions.

2. Meanwhile, in 10- by 6-inch baking dish, combine soup and milk. Add tuna, vegetables and cooked rice; stir gently to mix.

3. Bake 20 minutes or until hot and bubbling; stir. Makes 4 cups or 4 servings.

Meatball 'n' Green Bean Soup

$^1/_2$ pound bulk pork sausage
  Vegetable oil
2 medium onions, chopped
2 medium carrots, sliced
1 can (10$^3/_4$ ounces) Campbell's
  condensed golden
  mushroom soup

1 can (10$^1/_2$ ounces) Campbell's
  condensed chicken broth
2$^1/_2$ cups water
3 medium all-purpose potatoes,
  cut into $^3/_4$-inch pieces
1 cup frozen cut green beans
$^1/_8$ teaspoon pepper

1. Shape sausage into 16 (1-inch) meatballs. In 4-quart saucepan over
   medium heat, brown meatballs on all sides. Remove and drain on
   paper towels, reserving drippings in pan.

2. Add enough oil to pan drippings to make *1 tablespoon*, if necessary.
   Over medium heat, in hot drippings, cook onions and carrots
   3 minutes. Spoon off fat.

3. Stir in soup, broth, water, potatoes, green beans, pepper and
   cooked meatballs. Heat to boiling. Reduce heat to low. Cover;
   cook 10 minutes more or until potatoes and beans are tender.
   Makes 7$^1/_2$ cups or 5 servings.

Shrimp in Pastry Puffs

*For a special touch, sprinkle with a little snipped fresh parsley,
chives or watercress.*

6 frozen patty shells
2 tablespoons margarine
  or butter
2 cups sliced fresh mushrooms
1 can (10$^3/_4$ ounces) Campbell's
  condensed cream of
  celery soup

$^1/_4$ cup Chablis or other dry
  white wine
$^1/_2$ cup frozen peas
1$^1/_2$ pounds small shrimp, shelled
  and deveined

1. Preheat oven and bake patty shells according to package directions;
   keep warm.

2. Meanwhile, in 10-inch skillet over medium heat, in hot margarine,
   cook mushrooms until tender and liquid is evaporated, stirring
   occasionally.

3. Stir in soup, wine and peas. Reduce heat to low. Heat until boiling.
   Stir in shrimp; cook until shrimp turn pink and opaque. Spoon
   shrimp mixture over patty shells. Makes 5 cups or 6 servings.

Gingered Vegetables 〜〜〜

*Some of our taste-testers preferred this served on a bed of rice.
Pictured opposite.*

1 tablespoon vegetable oil
1 cup *each* diagonally sliced
   carrots, diagonally sliced
   celery, sweet red pepper
   strips, coarsely chopped
   onion, broccoli flowerets
   and snow peas

1 clove garlic, minced
$\frac{1}{2}$ teaspoon ground ginger
2 tablespoons cornstarch
1 can ($10\frac{1}{2}$ ounces) Campbell's
   condensed chicken broth

1. In 10-inch skillet or wok over high heat, in hot oil, stir-fry carrots, celery, red pepper and onion 3 minutes.

2. Add broccoli, snow peas, garlic and ginger. Sprinkle cornstarch over vegetables. Stir in broth. Cook until mixture boils and thickens, stirring often. Reduce heat to low. Cover; simmer until vegetables are tender-crisp.

3. Serve with *soy sauce*, if desired. Makes 4 cups or 4 servings.

To microwave: Omit oil. In 3-quart microwave-safe casserole, combine vegetables and garlic. Cover with lid; microwave on HIGH 7 minutes or until vegetables are tender-crisp, stirring once during cooking. Sprinkle cornstarch over vegetables. Stir in ginger and broth until blended. Cover; microwave on HIGH 4 minutes or until thickened, stirring once during cooking. Serve as directed in step 3.

*You can reduce the sodium in your meals by using a
reduced-sodium soy sauce.*

Gingered Vegetables

Curry-Sauced Cauliflower

A great make-ahead recipe—just reheat in your microwave oven.
Pictured opposite.

4 cups cauliflowerets
1 can (10¾ ounces) Campbell's
   condensed cream of celery
   soup
½ cup milk
½ cup shredded Cheddar cheese
   (2 ounces)

½ teaspoon curry powder
   Generous dash pepper
1 cup frozen peas, thawed
½ cup diced sweet red pepper
   Toasted sliced almonds
   for garnish

1. In covered 10-inch skillet over medium heat, in ½ inch boiling water, cook cauliflower 5 minutes or until tender-crisp. Drain in colander.

2. In same skillet, combine soup, milk, cheese, curry and pepper. Add cooked cauliflower, peas and red pepper. Over medium heat, cook 5 minutes or until vegetables are tender, stirring often. Garnish with almonds. Makes 5 cups or 10 servings.

To microwave: In 2-quart microwave-safe casserole, place cauliflower in ½ inch water. Cover with lid; microwave on HIGH 10 minutes or until tender-crisp. Drain in colander. In same casserole, stir soup, milk, cheese, curry and pepper until smooth. Add cooked cauliflower, peas and red pepper. Cover; microwave on HIGH 3 minutes or until vegetables are tender and cheese melts, stirring once during cooking. Garnish as directed in step 2.

Vegetables in Two Cheese-Beer Sauce

6 OR LESS

2 cups broccoli flowerets
2 cups cauliflowerets
1 can (11 ounces) Campbell's
   condensed Cheddar cheese
   soup/sauce

⅓ cup beer
1½ cups shredded Swiss cheese
   (6 ounces)
   Dash ground nutmeg

1. In covered 4-quart saucepan over medium heat, in 1 inch boiling water, cook broccoli and cauliflower 6 minutes or until tender. Drain in colander.

2. Meanwhile, in 2-quart saucepan, combine soup, beer, cheese and nutmeg. Over medium heat, heat through, stirring frequently.

3. On serving platter, arrange vegetables alternating broccoli and cauliflower to resemble a head of cauliflower. Pour sauce over vegetables. Makes 2 cups sauce for vegetables; 6 servings.

Curry-Sauced Cauliflower

Spicy Potatoes Olé 〰〰

These zesty potatoes taste terrific with broiled poultry or pork.

1 package (24 ounces) frozen
diced potatoes (5 cups)
2 tablespoons margarine
or butter
1 cup diced zucchini
½ teaspoon chili powder

1 can (11 ounces) Campbell's
condensed nacho cheese
soup/dip
1 can (8 ounces) whole kernel
corn, drained
½ cup shredded Monterey Jack
cheese (2 ounces)

1. In 3-quart saucepan over high heat, heat 1 quart salted water to
   boiling. Add potatoes. Return to boiling. Cook 2 minutes or until
   potatoes are tender. Drain in colander, reserving ½ *cup* of the
   cooking liquid; set aside.

2. In same saucepan over medium heat, in hot margarine, cook
   zucchini and chili powder 2 minutes, stirring often.

3. Stir in soup, corn, cheese, cooked potatoes and reserved ½ *cup*
   liquid. Cook 5 minutes or until heated through, stirring often. Serve
   with *sour cream*, if desired. Makes 6 cups or 8 servings.

To microwave: In 2-quart microwave-safe casserole, combine potatoes
and margarine. Cover with lid; microwave on HIGH 6 minutes or until
potatoes are tender, stirring once during heating. Stir in zucchini, chili
powder, soup and corn. Cover; microwave on HIGH 5 minutes or until
vegetables are tender. Sprinkle with cheese. Let stand, uncovered,
2 minutes. Serve as directed in step 3.

Quick Rice and Beans ◇EXTRA EASY◇

3 slices bacon, diced
1 clove garlic, minced
¼ teaspoon ground coriander
⅛ teaspoon ground cumin
1 cup regular rice, uncooked
½ cup drained canned chick
peas (garbanzo beans),
kidney beans or pinto beans

1 can (10½ ounces) Campbell's
condensed beef broth
½ cup water
1 bay leaf
Generous dash pepper

1. In 2-quart saucepan over medium-high heat, cook bacon until crisp.
   Add garlic, coriander and cumin. Cook 1 minute, stirring constantly.

2. Stir in rice, chick peas, broth, water, bay leaf and pepper. Heat to
   boiling. Reduce heat to low. Cover; simmer 20 minutes or until rice
   is done. Remove bay leaf; discard. Makes 4 cups or 8 servings.

Broccoli-Rice Casserole 〜〜〜

Serve at a family picnic or neighborhood potluck.

1 tablespoon vegetable oil
$\frac{1}{2}$ cup chopped celery
$\frac{1}{4}$ cup chopped onion
1 can (10$\frac{3}{4}$ ounces) Campbell's
   condensed cream of broccoli
   or cream of mushroom soup
$\frac{1}{4}$ cup milk
1 cup pasteurized process
   cheese spread cut in
   $\frac{1}{4}$-inch cubes

1 package (10 ounces) frozen
   chopped broccoli, thawed
   and drained
1 can (8 ounces) sliced water
   chestnuts, drained
2 cups cooked regular rice
Paprika

1. Preheat oven to 350°F. In 1$\frac{1}{2}$-quart saucepan over medium heat, in hot oil, cook celery and onion until tender-crisp, stirring occasionally. Stir in soup and milk.

2. In 10- by 6-inch baking dish, place cheese, broccoli, water chestnuts and rice. Stir in soup mixture. Sprinkle with paprika. Bake 30 minutes or until bubbling. Makes 5 cups or 8 servings.

To microwave: Omit oil. In 10- by 6-inch microwave-safe baking dish, combine celery and onion. Cover with vented plastic wrap; microwave on HIGH 3 minutes. Stir in soup and milk. Add cheese, broccoli, water chestnuts and rice, stirring gently to mix. Sprinkle with paprika. Microwave, uncovered, on HIGH 10 minutes, rotating dish halfway through cooking.

Squash 'n' Macaroni in Spicy Cheese Sauce

6 ounces corkscrew macaroni,
   uncooked
2 tablespoons margarine
   or butter
4 cups sliced zucchini or yellow
   squash
$\frac{1}{4}$ cup sliced green onions
1 clove garlic, minced

$\frac{1}{2}$ teaspoon ground cumin
1 can (11 ounces) Campbell's
   condensed Cheddar cheese
   soup/sauce
$\frac{1}{2}$ cup milk
$\frac{1}{2}$ cup shredded Cheddar cheese
   (2 ounces)

1. Cook macaroni according to package directions; drain. In 3-quart saucepan over medium heat, in hot margarine, cook squash, green onions, garlic and cumin 5 minutes or until squash is tender-crisp, stirring often.

2. Stir in soup, milk and cheese. Heat until cheese melts. Stir in drained macaroni; heat through. Makes 6 cups or 6 servings.

Peas and Carrots in Thyme Sauce

Even kids will love this sophisticated version of peas and carrots.
Serve with mini hamburgers as shown. Pictured opposite.

1 tablespoon margarine
   or butter
1 small onion, chopped
¼ teaspoon dried thyme leaves,
   crushed
1 can (10¾ ounces) Campbell's
   condensed cream of celery
   soup

⅓ cup milk
   Generous dash pepper
1 bag (16 ounces) frozen peas
1 cup carrots cut into 2-inch
   julienne strips

1. In 2-quart saucepan over medium heat, in hot margarine, cook
   onion and thyme until onion is tender, stirring occasionally.

2. Stir in soup, milk and pepper. Add peas and carrots. Heat to boiling.
   Reduce heat to low. Cover; simmer 8 minutes or until vegetables are
   tender, stirring occasionally. Makes 3½ cups or 4 servings.

Broccoli Bake 〰〰 🅖 OR LESS ◇EXTRA EASY◇

2 packages (10 ounces *each*)
   frozen broccoli spears or 1
   package (20 ounces) frozen
   broccoli cuts
1 can (10¾ ounces) Campbell's
   condensed cream of broccoli
   or cream of mushroom soup

½ cup milk
1 teaspoon soy sauce
   Dash pepper
1 can (2.8 ounces) French-
   fried onions, divided

1. Preheat oven to 350°F. Cook broccoli according to package
   directions; drain.

2. Meanwhile, in small bowl, combine soup, milk, soy sauce and
   pepper. In 10- by 6-inch baking dish, layer *half* of the broccoli,
   half of the soup mixture and *half* of the onions. Top with remaining
   broccoli and the soup mixture. Bake 25 minutes.

3. Top with remaining onions. Bake 5 minutes more. Makes 6 servings.

To microwave: Prepare as directed *except* use a 10- by 6-inch
microwave-safe baking dish. Cover with waxed paper; microwave on
HIGH 8 minutes, rotating dish halfway through heating. Top with
remaining onions. Microwave, uncovered, on HIGH 1 minute more.

Peas and Carrots in Thyme Sauce

Mixed Vegetable Pilaf

Pictured opposite along with ham, cranberry sauce and green beans.

2 tablespoons margarine
  or butter
1 cup sliced fresh mushrooms
$\frac{1}{4}$ teaspoon dried basil leaves,
  crushed
1 can (10$\frac{1}{2}$ ounces) Campbell's
  condensed chicken broth

$\frac{3}{4}$ cup water
1 cup regular rice, uncooked
1 small zucchini, halved
  lengthwise and sliced
$\frac{1}{2}$ cup shredded carrot

1. In 10-inch skillet over medium heat, in hot margarine, cook mushrooms and basil 3 minutes, stirring occasionally.

2. Add broth and water. Heat to boiling. Stir in rice. Return to boiling. Reduce heat to low. Cover; simmer 15 minutes.

3. Stir in zucchini and carrot. Cover; simmer 5 minutes. Remove from heat. Let stand, covered, 5 minutes before serving. Makes about 5 cups or 6 servings.

Mushrooms in Garlic-Herb Sauce

Toss with hot cooked pasta or spooned over grilled meats.

2 tablespoons olive oil
1 medium onion, finely
  chopped
4 cloves garlic, minced
$\frac{1}{4}$ teaspoon dried rosemary
  leaves, crushed
$\frac{1}{4}$ teaspoon dried thyme leaves,
  crushed
1$\frac{1}{2}$ pounds fresh mushrooms,
  thinly sliced

1 can (10$\frac{1}{2}$ ounces) Campbell's
  condensed French onion
  soup
1 teaspoon lime or lemon juice
$\frac{1}{4}$ cup Chablis or other dry
  white wine
Chopped fresh parsley for
  garnish

1. In 10-inch skillet over medium heat, in hot oil, cook onion, garlic, rosemary and thyme until onion is tender, stirring occasionally.

2. Increase heat to medium-high. Add mushrooms. Cook until mushrooms just begin to brown, stirring occasionally. Add soup and lime juice. Heat to boiling. Reduce heat to low. Simmer until mushrooms are just tender, stirring occasionally.

3. Add wine. Simmer 3 minutes. Garnish with parsley. Makes 2$\frac{3}{4}$ cups or 6 servings.

Mixed Vegetable Pilaf

Cheese-Sauced Summer Vegetables

Look for fresh sugar snap peas when in season—they cook to perfection in only 5 minutes.

3 tablespoons margarine
  or butter
1 medium zucchini or yellow
  squash, halved lengthwise
  and sliced
1 cup sliced fresh mushrooms
1 clove garlic, minced
¼ teaspoon dried basil leaves,
  crushed

1 can (11 ounces) Campbell's
  condensed Cheddar cheese
  soup/sauce
½ cup milk
1 package (8 ounces) frozen
  sugar snap peas (2 cups)
⅛ teaspoon pepper
1 cup cherry tomatoes *each*
  cut in half

1. In 3-quart saucepan over medium heat, in hot margarine, cook zucchini 2 minutes, stirring occasionally. Transfer to bowl.

2. In same saucepan over medium heat, cook mushrooms, garlic and basil 2 minutes, stirring occasionally.

3. Stir soup and milk into saucepan. Add peas and pepper. Heat to boiling. Reduce heat to low. Cover; simmer 5 minutes or until peas are tender, stirring often.

4. Stir in tomatoes and cooked zucchini. Heat through. Makes 4 cups or 6 servings.

Curried Peanut Rice *EXTRA EASY*

Just the right accompaniment to your favorite Chinese stir-fry.

2 tablespoons vegetable oil
¼ cup sliced green onions
2 teaspoons curry powder
1 can (10½ ounces) Campbell's
  condensed chicken broth

½ cup frozen peas
1¼ cups quick-cooking rice,
  uncooked
½ cup coarsely chopped
  unsalted roasted peanuts

1. In 2-quart saucepan over medium heat, in hot oil, cook green onions and curry powder until onions are tender, stirring occasionally.

2. Add broth and peas. Heat to boiling. Add rice. Remove from heat. Cover; let stand 5 minutes or until most of the liquid is absorbed. Stir in peanuts. Fluff with fork before serving. Makes 2½ cups or 5 servings.

Savory Parslied Rice ◆EXTRA EASY◆

For a spicier rice, stir in a chopped seeded jalapeño pepper and use the whole can of green chilies.

1 tablespoon margarine
   or butter
½ cup finely chopped onion
2 cloves garlic, minced
1 can (10½ ounces) Campbell's
   condensed chicken broth

1¼ cups quick-cooking rice,
   uncooked
3 tablespoons chopped
   green chilies
¼ cup chopped fresh parsley

1. In 2-quart saucepan over medium heat, in hot margarine, cook onion and garlic until onion is tender, stirring occasionally.

2. Add broth. Heat to boiling. Add rice and green chilies. Remove from heat. Cover; let stand 5 minutes or until most of the liquid is absorbed. Stir in parsley. Fluff with fork before serving. Makes 3 cups or 6 servings.

Vegetable Couscous

Reheat leftover vegetable couscous in your microwave oven. Stir in 1 or 2 tablespoons water, if needed.

1 can (10½ ounces) Campbell's
   condensed chicken broth
1½ cups couscous, uncooked
¼ cup vegetable oil
1 cup sliced fresh mushrooms
1 cup chopped onions

1 cup shredded carrots
1 tablespoon grated fresh ginger
2 cloves garlic, minced
1 tablespoon soy sauce
1 tablespoon lemon juice

1. In 2-quart saucepan over high heat, heat broth to boiling. Remove from heat. Stir in couscous. Cover; let stand 5 minutes.

2. Meanwhile, in 10-inch skillet over medium heat, in hot oil, cook mushrooms, onions, carrots, ginger and garlic until vegetables are tender-crisp, stirring often. Stir in soy sauce and lemon juice.

3. Add couscous. Heat through. Makes 5 cups or 10 servings.

Bulgur with Basil and Walnuts

If fresh basil is available, finely chop enough to make 1 tablespoon and stir in with the walnuts.

1 can (10½ ounces) Campbell's
   condensed chicken broth
1 medium onion, chopped
2 tablespoons margarine
   or butter
1 clove garlic, minced

1 teaspoon dried basil leaves,
   crushed
1¼ cups bulgur wheat, uncooked
⅓ cup chopped walnuts
1 tablespoon lemon juice

1. In 2-quart saucepan over medium heat, combine broth, onion, margarine, garlic and basil. Heat to boiling.

2. Add remaining ingredients. Remove from heat. Cover; let stand 15 minutes or until liquid is absorbed. Makes about 4 cups or 8 servings.

Summer Garden Soup 〰️

If fresh basil isn't available, use ½ teaspoon crushed dried basil— just add it before the soup simmers. Pictured opposite.

1 can (10½ ounces) Campbell's
   condensed chicken broth
⅔ cup water
½ cup zucchini cut in 2-inch
   julienne strips
½ cup seeded and chopped
   tomato

½ cup frozen whole kernel corn
⅓ cup chopped carrot
¼ cup chopped onion
1½ teaspoons chopped fresh
   basil leaves

In 2-quart saucepan over high heat, combine all ingredients *except* fresh basil. Heat to boiling. Reduce heat to low. Simmer 10 minutes or until vegetables are tender, stirring occasionally. Stir in basil. Makes 3 cups or 3 servings.

To microwave: In 1½-quart microwave-safe casserole, combine all ingredients *except* fresh basil. Cover with lid; microwave on HIGH 12 minutes or until vegetables are tender, stirring twice during cooking. Stir in basil.

Summer Garden Soup

Quick Gazpacho ◆EXTRA EASY◆

Tomato soup is the base for this fast-fixin' soup. Pictured opposite.

1 can (10¾ ounces) Campbell's
  condensed tomato soup
1 soup can water
1 tablespoon wine vinegar
1 teaspoon olive oil
1 clove garlic, minced
¼ teaspoon dried basil leaves,
  crushed

1 cup seeded and chopped
  cucumber
½ cup chopped sweet red or
  green pepper
1 tablespoon chopped onion
  Fresh basil leaves for garnish

1. In medium bowl, stir soup until smooth. Stir in water, vinegar, oil, garlic and dried basil; blend well. Stir in cucumber, red pepper and onion. Cover; refrigerate until serving time, at least 6 hours.

2. Serve in chilled bowls. Garnish with fresh basil. Makes 3½ cups or 4 servings.

Hint-of-Mint Pea Soup

Fresh mint can be easily grown in your kitchen window.

1 can (10¾ ounces) Campbell's
  condensed cream of potato
  soup
1 can (10½ ounces) Campbell's
  condensed chicken broth
1 package (10 ounces) frozen
  peas
1 tablespoon lemon juice

¼ teaspoon dried mint leaves,
  crushed, or ¾ teaspoon
  chopped fresh mint leaves
⅛ teaspoon ground white pepper
½ cup milk
  Fresh mint leaves for garnish
  Chopped walnuts for garnish

1. In 2-quart saucepan, combine soup and broth, stirring until smooth. Add peas. Over medium heat, heat to boiling. Reduce heat to low. Cover; simmer 8 minutes or until peas are tender.

2. In covered blender or food processor, blend soup mixture, lemon juice, ¼ teaspoon dried mint and the pepper until smooth. Return mixture to saucepan.

3. Gradually stir in milk. Over medium heat, heat through. Garnish with fresh mint and walnuts. Makes 4 cups or 4 servings.

Quick Gazpacho

Watercress Potato Soup 🥣 OR LESS

This is also delicious served cold like classic vichyssoise. Just refrigerate at least 4 hours before serving.

1 tablespoon margarine
  or butter
$\frac{1}{2}$ cup chopped onion
2 cups chopped watercress
$1\frac{1}{2}$ cups water

1 can (10¾ ounces) Campbell's
  condensed cream of potato
  soup
$\frac{1}{8}$ teaspoon ground nutmeg
Watercress for garnish

1. In $1\frac{1}{2}$-quart saucepan over medium heat, in hot margarine, cook onion and watercress until onion is tender, stirring occasionally. Add water. Heat to boiling. Reduce heat to low. Cover; simmer 10 minutes. Drain mixture, reserving liquid. Set aside.

2. In covered blender or food processor, blend watercress mixture until almost smooth. Add soup; blend until smooth. Add reserved liquid and nutmeg; blend until smooth. Return to saucepan; heat through. Garnish with watercress. Makes 3 cups or 4 servings.

South-of-the-Border Onion Soup ◇EXTRA EASY◇

For added zip, top this speedy soup with a spoonful of sour cream and some shredded Monterey Jack cheese with chilies.

1 can (10½ ounces) Campbell's
  condensed French onion
  soup
1 soup can water
$\frac{1}{2}$ cup whole kernel corn

$\frac{1}{2}$ cup chopped seeded tomato
2 tablespoons chopped green
  chilies
1 tablespoon lime juice
$\frac{1}{4}$ teaspoon ground cumin

In 2-quart saucepan, combine all ingredients. Over medium heat, heat to boiling. Reduce heat to low. Simmer 10 minutes. Makes 4 cups or 4 servings.

Southwest Potato Soup

1 tablespoon margarine
   or butter
½ cup chopped green onions
1 can (10¾ ounces) Campbell's
   condensed cream of potato
   soup
1½ cups milk
¼ cup shredded Monterey Jack
   cheese with chilies
   (1 ounce)

1. In 2-quart saucepan over medium heat, in hot margarine, cook
   green onions until tender, stirring occasionally.

2. Add soup and milk; stir until blended. Heat through. Remove from
   heat. Add cheese, stirring until cheese melts. Makes about 2¾ cups
   or 3 servings.

Double Clam Chowder

1 can (10¾ ounces) Campbell's
   condensed cream of celery
   soup
1 can (10¾ ounces) Campbell's
   condensed New England
   clam chowder
1 can (6½ ounces) chopped
   clams, undrained
1 soup can milk
1 soup can water
   Chopped fresh parsley
   for garnish

In 2-quart saucepan over medium heat, combine all ingredients *except*
parsley. Heat through, stirring occasionally. *Do not boil.* Garnish with
parsley. Makes about 5½ cups or 5 servings.

Down-Home Vegetable Chowder

*For added flavor, sprinkle crumbled bacon, chopped green onion
tops and chopped sweet red pepper on each serving.*

2 tablespoons margarine
   or butter
¼ cup sliced green onions
½ cup sliced celery
1 can (10¾ ounces) Campbell's
   condensed cream of
   potato soup
1 soup can milk
1 cup frozen whole kernel corn
⅛ teaspoon pepper

In 2-quart saucepan over medium heat, in hot margarine, cook green
onions and celery until tender, stirring occasionally. Add soup, milk,
corn and pepper. Heat through, stirring often. Makes 3½ cups or
3 servings.

Dilled Salmon Dip

Look for mini zucchini, eggplant and summer squash to add to your assortment of fresh vegetable dippers. Pictured opposite.

1 can (10¾ ounces) Campbell's condensed cream of celery soup
¼ cup mayonnaise or sour cream
2 tablespoons prepared horseradish

1 tablespoon chopped fresh dill or 1 teaspoon dried dill weed, crushed
⅛ teaspoon pepper
1 can (7½ ounces) salmon, drained and flaked
Fresh chopped dill and dill sprig for garnish

1. In medium bowl, combine soup, mayonnaise, horseradish, 1 tablespoon chopped dill and the pepper; mix well. Add salmon; mix lightly. Cover; chill 15 minutes.

2. Garnish dip as desired. Serve with *assorted cut-up vegetables* and *party rye bread* for dipping. Makes 2 cups.

Middle Eastern-Style Dip

1 can (15 ounces) chick peas (garbanzo beans), drained
1 can (10¾ ounces) Campbell's condensed cream of celery soup
½ cup chopped blanched almonds, toasted

3 tablespoons lemon juice
2 cloves garlic, minced
1 tablespoon olive oil
Generous dash ground red pepper

In covered blender or food processor, combine all ingredients. Blend until smooth. Serve at room temperature or chilled with *pita bread, cut-up fresh vegetables* or *crackers* for dipping. Makes 2¼ cups.

> *To toast chopped almonds in microwave oven,* spread in a single layer on a plain white paper towel. Microwave on HIGH 1½ minutes, stirring once during cooking.

Dilled Salmon Dip

Curried Peanut Dip

1 can (10¾ ounces) Campbell's
    condensed cream of chicken
    soup
¾ cup plain yogurt

¼ cup chunky peanut butter
2 teaspoons curry powder
Chopped peanuts for garnish

In small bowl, combine all ingredients. Serve at room temperature or
chilled. Garnish with peanuts. Serve with wedges of *fresh pears* and
apples for dipping. Makes 2 cups.

> ***To keep fruit, such as pears and apples, from browning,*** *dip into
> lemon juice or ascorbic acid color keeper after cutting.*

Artichoke-Chili Dip

*Our souper version of the popular hot artichoke dip that's
made with mayonnaise.*

1 can (10¾ ounces) Campbell's
    condensed cream of celery
    soup
2 packages (3 ounces *each*)
    cream cheese, softened
1 can (14 ounces) artichoke
    hearts, rinsed, drained
    and chopped

1 can (4 ounces) chopped
    green chilies
½ cup grated Parmesan cheese
    Paprika

1. Preheat oven to 375°F.

2. Meanwhile, in 1-quart casserole, stir soup and cream cheese
   until smooth. Stir in artichokes, chilies and Parmesan. Sprinkle
   with paprika.

3. Bake 15 minutes or until hot and bubbling. Serve with *crackers*
   or *tortilla chips* for dipping. Makes 3½ cups.

To microwave: In 1½-quart microwave-safe casserole, stir soup and
cream cheese until smooth. Stir in artichokes, chilies and Parmesan.
Microwave, uncovered, on HIGH 6 minutes or until hot, stirring twice
during cooking. Sprinkle with paprika. Serve as directed in step 3.

Hot Cheese and Sausage Dip

For added zip, use hot Italian sausage.

¼ pound Italian sausage, casing removed, bulk pork sausage or ground raw turkey
⅓ cup chopped green onions

1 can (11 ounces) Campbell's condensed Cheddar cheese soup/sauce
½ cup water
Chopped green onions for garnish

1. In 1½-quart saucepan over medium heat, cook sausage and green onions 4 minutes or until sausage is browned, stirring to separate meat. Spoon off fat.

2. Stir in soup and water. Heat until hot and bubbling, stirring occasionally. Pour into heated serving dish or fondue pot. Garnish with green onions. Serve with *celery sticks, carrot sticks, bagel chips* or *tortilla chips* for dipping. Makes about 2 cups.

Turkey Meatballs in Mushroom Sauce

To save time, precooked beef meatballs can be purchased at your grocery store—look in the deli or freezer sections.

1 pound ground raw turkey
½ cup quick-cooking oats
¼ cup chopped onion
¼ cup chopped fresh parsley
1 egg, beaten
¼ teaspoon pepper
2 tablespoons vegetable oil

1 can (10¾ ounces) Campbell's condensed golden mushroom soup
½ cup water
Chopped fresh parsley for garnish

1. In medium bowl, combine turkey, oats, onion, parsley, egg and pepper; mix lightly but well. Shape mixture into 30 (1-inch) meatballs.

2. In 10-inch skillet over medium heat, in hot oil, cook meatballs until browned on all sides. Spoon off fat.

3. Stir in soup and water. Heat to boiling. Reduce heat to low. Cover; simmer 20 minutes. Garnish with parsley. Serve with cocktail picks. Makes 30 meatballs.

Cheddar Swiss Fondue 〰〰

Along with the bread dippers, serve assorted fresh fruit.
Pictured opposite.

1 tablespoon margarine or butter	¼ cup Chablis or other dry white wine
½ cup chopped onion	1 teaspoon caraway seed
1 clove garlic, minced	2 cups shredded Swiss cheese
1 can (11 ounces) Campbell's condensed Cheddar cheese soup/sauce	(8 ounces)

1. In 2-quart saucepan over medium heat, in hot margarine, cook onion and garlic 10 minutes, stirring often.

2. Stir in soup, wine and caraway seed. Gradually add cheese, stirring until smooth after each addition.

3. Pour cheese mixture into heated serving dish or fondue pot. Serve with *pumpernickel* or *French bread cubes* for dipping. Makes 2⅓ cups.

To microwave: In 2-quart microwave-safe casserole, combine margarine, onion and garlic. Cover with lid; microwave on HIGH 3 to 4 minutes or until onion is tender, stirring once. Stir in soup, wine, caraway seed and cheese. Cover; microwave on HIGH 4 to 6 minutes or until cheese melts, stirring twice during cooking. Serve as directed in step 3.

Souper-Easy Cheese Dip 〰〰 *EXTRA EASY*

1 can (11 ounces) Campbell's condensed Cheddar cheese soup/sauce	2 tablespoons chili sauce 2 tablespoons milk

In 1-quart saucepan, combine all ingredients; mix well. Over medium heat, heat until mixture is smooth, stirring often. Serve dip with *corn chips* or as a topper over *French-fried potatoes or potato skins*. Makes 1¼ cups.

To microwave: In 1-quart microwave-safe casserole, combine all ingredients; stir well. Cover with lid; microwave on HIGH 4 minutes or until hot, stirring twice during heating. Serve as directed above.

Cheddar Swiss Fondue

Potato Skin Nachos

2 packages (20 ounces *each*)
  frozen potato skins
1 can (11 ounces) Campbell's
  condensed nacho cheese
  soup/dip

¼ cup milk
½ cup sliced pitted ripe olives
½ cup chopped sweet red pepper
  or seeded tomato
¼ cup chopped green onions

1. Prepare frozen potato skins according to package directions; keep warm.

2. Meanwhile, in 1½-quart saucepan over medium heat, combine soup and milk. Heat through, stirring occasionally.

3. Spoon sauce over prepared potato skins. Sprinkle with olives, red pepper and green onions. Makes about 24 appetizers.

Chipped Beef in French Rolls

This sauce is also good spooned into hot potato skin shells.

9 French rolls (*each* 2½ by
  2 inches long), halved
  lengthwise
1 can (10¾ ounces) Campbell's
  condensed cream of
  mushroom soup
1 package (3 ounces) cream
  cheese, softened

3 tablespoons chopped
  green onion
2 ounces dried beef, chopped,
  rinsed and well drained
¼ teaspoon pepper
Chopped fresh parsley
  for garnish

1. Preheat oven to 450°F. Using tines of a fork, pull out some of the centers of roll (about 1 tablespoon), forming shells ½ inch thick. Place shells on baking sheet. Bake 5 to 6 minutes or until golden and crisp.

2. Meanwhile, in 10-inch skillet, combine remaining ingredients *except* parsley. Over medium heat, heat 5 minutes or until heated through, stirring occasionally.

3. Divide hot filling among toasted bread shells, using 1 heaping tablespoon for each. Garnish with parsley. Makes 18 appetizers.

To microwave: Prepare bread shells and bake as directed in step 1. In 1-quart microwave-safe casserole, combine remaining ingredients *except* parsley. Cover with lid; microwave on HIGH 5 minutes or until hot and bubbling, stirring twice during cooking. Serve as directed in step 3.

Mexican-Style Appetizers

To make this recipe even easier, arrange the chips on a platter, pour the hot cheese mixture over and serve.

2 tablespoons vegetable oil
4 green onions, finely chopped
2 cloves garlic, minced
1 can (15 ounces) tomatoes, drained, cut up
1 can (11 ounces) Campbell's condensed nacho cheese soup/dip

1 bag (7 ounces) round corn tortilla chips (about 50)
Chopped pickled jalapeño peppers for garnish
Sliced pitted ripe olives for garnish

1. In 10-inch skillet over medium heat, in hot oil, cook green onions and garlic 1 minute, stirring constantly. Add tomatoes; cook 2 minutes. Gradually stir in soup. Heat 5 minutes or until heated through, stirring occasionally.

2. Spread *1 heaping teaspoon* of the soup mixture on each tortilla chip. Garnish with jalapeño peppers and olives. Makes 50 appetizers.

Cheddar Cheese Dipping Sauce

Also delicious served with French fries or tater tots.

1 can (11 ounces) Campbell's condensed Cheddar cheese soup/sauce
½ cup water
2 to 3 tablespoons sweet pickle relish

1 tablespoon ketchup
¼ teaspoon dry mustard
¼ teaspoon garlic powder
⅛ teaspoon pepper

In 2-quart saucepan, combine all ingredients. Over medium heat, heat 5 to 7 minutes or until heated through, stirring occasionally. Serve with hot *cocktail franks, sliced knockwurst, kielbasa chunks, cherry tomatoes* or *French bread cubes* for dipping. Makes 1⅔ cups sauce.

To microwave: Reduce water to ⅓ *cup.* In 1-quart microwave-safe casserole, combine all ingredients. Cover with lid; microwave on HIGH 4 minutes or until hot and bubbling, stirring once during cooking. Serve as directed above.

Mini Broccoli Pizzas

These individual broccoli pizzas are easy to assemble. Choose from a variety of toppers such as: sliced pepperoni, chopped artichoke hearts, chopped shrimp, sliced green onions and sliced olives. Pictured opposite and on back cover.

2 cups small broccoli flowerets
$\frac{1}{2}$ cup sweet red pepper cut
   in strips
1 can (10$\frac{3}{4}$ ounces) Campbell's
   condensed cream of
   broccoli soup
$\frac{1}{4}$ teaspoon garlic powder

$\frac{1}{4}$ teaspoon dried Italian
   seasoning, crushed
6 English muffins, split
   and toasted
2 cups shredded mozzarella
   cheese (8 ounces)

1. Preheat oven to 375°F.

2. Meanwhile, in small saucepan over high heat, in boiling water, cook broccoli and red pepper 3 minutes. Drain well; set aside.

3. In small bowl, combine soup, garlic and Italian seasoning. Spread soup mixture evenly over 12 muffin halves; place on baking sheets. Top each with cooked broccoli and red pepper. Sprinkle with cheese. Bake 10 minutes or until cheese melts. Serve immediately. Makes 12 mini pizzas.

Cheese 'n' Crab Appetizers

6 OR LESS   *EXTRA EASY*

1 can (11 ounces) Campbell's
   condensed Cheddar cheese
   soup/sauce
2 tablespoons chopped green
   onion
1 tablespoon chopped pimento

1 teaspoon Louisiana-style
   hot sauce
2 cans (6 ounces *each*) crab
   meat, drained
6 English muffins, split
   and toasted

1. In medium bowl, combine soup, green onion, pimento and hot sauce. Fold in crab meat. Spread soup mixture evenly over 12 muffin halves; place on baking sheets.

2. Broil 6 inches from heat 5 to 6 minutes or until hot and lightly browned. Quarter each muffin half for appetizers or serve as 12 open-face sandwiches. Makes 48 appetizers or 12 open-face sandwiches.

Mini Broccoli Pizzas

Eggs
  Cheesy Mushroom Frittata, 44
  Classic Campbelled Eggs, 14
  Fiesta Eggs, 46
  Sausage Stuffing Broccoli Bake, 59

Fettuccine with Mushroom-Clam
  Sauce, 12
Fiesta Eggs, 46
Fish
  Broccoli Fish Chowder, 27
  Calico Tuna-Rice Bake, 64
  Cheesy Tuna and Twists, 27
  Cod Steaks Oriental, 12
  Creamy Dill Salmon Steaks, 26
  Dijon Cod Fillets, 25
  Dilled Salmon Dip, 85
  Fish with Swiss Cheese Sauce, 26
  Salsa Swordfish, 25
  Tuna-Tortellini Soup, 18

Garden-Style Vegetable Bisque, 34
Garlic Orange Beef, 38
German-Style Pork Stew, 60
Gingered Vegetables, 67
Ground Beef
  Beef Ziti Casserole, 64
  Cheeseburger Pizza, 36
  Cincinnati Chili, 39
  Hamburger 'n' Fixings Sandwiches, 15
  Hearty Sausage 'n' Cabbage Soup, 47
  Meatball Mushroom Sandwiches, 36
  Pineapple Beef Curry, 40
  Southwest Mac and Beef, 40
  Speedy Spicy Chili, 11
  Taco Salad, 42
  Tamale Pie, 58
  Zesty Spinach Meat Loaves, 62

Ham
  Chicken-Broccoli Cordon Bleu, 56
  Country Ham 'n' Potato Soup, 23
  Ham Barley Soup, 59
Hamburger 'n' Fixings Sandwiches, 15
Hearty Sausage 'n' Cabbage Soup, 47
Hint-of-Mint Pea Soup, 80
Hot Cheese and Sausage Dip, 87

Knockwurst Potato Chowder, 20

Lamb Stew, Winter, 62
Lemon-Broccoli Chicken, 28

Macaroni Ratatouille Soup, 58
Mandarin Chicken, 33
Meatball 'n' Green Bean Soup, 65
Meatball Mushroom Sandwiches, 36
Mexican-Style Appetizers, 91

Middle Eastern-Style Dip, 85
Mini Broccoli Pizzas, 92
Mixed Vegetable Pilaf, 74
Mushrooms in Garlic-Herb Sauce, 74

Nacho Chicken Tostadas, 8
Nacho Pork Chili, 60

Pasta
  Bavarian Kielbasa with Noodles, 44
  Bean-and-Bacon Mac Skillet, 39
  Beef Ziti Casserole, 64
  Cheesy Tuna and Twists, 27
  Fettuccine with Mushroom-Clam
    Sauce, 12
  Macaroni Ratatouille Soup, 58
  Saucy Cheese Tortellini, 14
  Souper Chicken Tetrazzini, 33
  Southwest Mac and Beef, 40
  Squash 'n' Macaroni in Spicy Cheese
    Sauce, 71
  Tuna-Tortellini Soup, 18
Peas and Carrots in Thyme Sauce, 72
Pepperoni Pizza Soup, 16
Philadelphia Cheesesteak Soup, 23
Pineapple Beef Curry, 40
Piquant Pork Chops, 38
Pork
  German-Style Pork Stew, 60
  Nacho Pork Chili, 60
  Piquant Pork Chops, 38
  Skillet Black-Eyed Peas 'n' Rice, 10
  Szechuan Shredded Pork, 11
Potato Skin Nachos, 90

Quick Gazpacho, 80
Quick Rice and Beans, 70

Reuben-Style Skillet, 15

Salsa Swordfish, 25
Sandwiches
  Cheeseburger Pizza, 36
  Chipped Beef in French Rolls, 90
  Hamburger 'n' Fixings
    Sandwiches, 15
  Meatball Mushroom Sandwiches, 36
  Mini Broccoli Pizzas, 92
Saucy Cheese Tortellini, 14
Sausage
  Bavarian Kielbasa with Noodles, 44
  Hearty Sausage 'n' Cabbage
    Soup, 47
  Hot Cheese and Sausage Dip, 87
  Knockwurst Potato Chowder, 20
  Macaroni Ratatouille Soup, 58
  Meatball 'n' Green Bean Soup, 65
  continued